GEBIR

WALTER SAVAGE LANDOR

Gebir

with "Crysaor"
& "The Phocæans"

EMPYREAN SERIES · SUBLUNARY EDITIONS · SEATTLE, WA

EMPYREAN SERIES No. 24

about

Gebir; a Poem: in Seven Books was first published in 1798 and published in revised form in 1803 and in 1831. "The Story of Crysaor" and "The Phocæans" first appeared in *Poetry by the Author of Gebir, and a Postscript to That Poem* (1802). The poem "Apology for *Gebir*" was first published in *The Examiner*, September 9, 1854.

This text of *Gebir* is faithful to the edition of 1803. The texts of "Crysaor", "The Phocæans", "Postscript to *Gebir*", and "Apology for *Gebir*" follow those printed in *The Poetical Works of Walter Savage Landor*, ed. Stephen Wheeler, Volumes 1 and 2, Oxford UP, 1937.

A digital supplement to this volume is available at: *sublunaryeditions.com/products/gebir-walter-savage-landor/*.

isbn

978-1-955190-60-2

CONTENTS

Introduction

*Far from soliciting the attention of those who are
passing by,* Gebir *is confined, I believe, to the
shop of one bookseller, and I never heard that he
had even made his appearance at the window.*
LANDOR, POSTSCRIPT TO *GEBIR*, 1800

This volume's modest ambition is to restore to adventurous readers three of Walter Savage Landor's most daring,
fascinating, and earliest works: "The Phocæans", *Gebir*,
and "Crysaor". Composed in an epic mode in blank verse
during the years 1795–1800 when Landor was in his early
twenties, these poems share a number of common elements, from their inspiration taken from ancient legends,
to their setting in the Mediterranean region (especially
Iberia), to their thematic coding of their author's political
attitudes with respect to kingship and tyranny. In this
prefatory note, I would like to supply some context that
might prove useful to readers unfamiliar with these works
or their publication history. While my aim is to be brief,
readers are invited to consult additional commentaries
on each of the three poems, which I have published at

their respective English Wikipedia pages.[1]

Let us begin with a loose chronology of the poems' composition.[2] Landor likely began work on "The Phocæans" in 1795, the year after which he was rusticated from Oxford for discharging a firearm indoors. It is likely that his work on this poem substantially ceased when, in the fall of 1796, he began work on *Gebir*. By 1798, *Gebir* was complete, although it would continue to be revised in English and also fully conceived in a parallel Latin version in the following years. "Crysaor" was likely written only after *Gebir* was brought to its first completion. It was certainly finalized by 1800.

The first of these three compositions to be offered for sale, likely in July or August of 1798, was *Gebir; A Poem, in Seven Books*. It bears noting that this date falls squarely between two events that are significant to English literature and to Landor's own political attitudes: namely, Napoleon's siege of Alexandria and imperialist invasion of Egypt,

1. *https://en.wikipedia.org/wiki/Gebir_(poem)/*
   https://en.wikipedia.org/wiki/Crysaor_(poem)/
   https://en.wikipedia.org/wiki/The_Phocæans_(poem)/

2. As Landor's own statements regarding the circumstances of the poems' composition are in some respects inconsistent and contradictory, it is not possible to establish a chronology with absolute certainty. Nor is there total agreement among Landor's critics and biographers. I here follow the approximate chronology given by William Bradley in *The Early Poems of Walter Savage Landor* (London: Bradbury, Agnew, & Co, 1913). Bradley's book provides an excellent in-depth commentary to the poems in this volume and is available at Internet Archive.

begun on July 1; and the publication in September of *Lyrical Ballads* by Samuel Taylor Coleridge and William Wordsworth, generally taken to coincide with the onset of the Romantic period in English literature.

Young though he was, *Gebir* was not Landor's first book; three years earlier, at the age of twenty, Landor had had printed and published—and very soon after, ordered to be withdrawn from sale—*The Poems of Walter Savage Landor* (June 1795). *Gebir; A Poem in Seven Books* on the other hand was published anonymously in the form of an unassuming paperbound pamphlet. Landor had found the subject for his poem in a book which his friend Rose Aylmer had loaned to him while he was living in South Wales between Swansea and Tenby. This book was *The Progress of Romance* (1785) by Clara Reeve, and it contained "The History of Charoba, Queen of Ægypt".[3] This story was in effect the translation of a translation of a story featuring in a manuscript by the medieval Arabic writer Murtadá Ibn al-'Afíf (1154–June 5, 1237).[4] In Reeve's version of the

3. Reeve's text is available as a digital supplement to this volume at *sublunaryeditions.com/gebir-walter-savage-landor/*. The digital supplement also contains Stanley T. Williams's scholarly essay "The Story of *Gebir*" (*PMLA*, 1921), a valuable but flawed commentary.

4. Rāġib, Yūsuf. "L'auteur de L'Égypte de Murtadi Fils Du Gaphiphe." *Arabica*, vol. 21, no. 2, 1974, pp. 203–09. Murtadá's medieval manuscript was translated into French by Pierre Vattier and published in 1666 and has been variously referred to in English as *The Egyptian History* and *The Marvels of Egypt*. The Arabic manuscript is no longer extant and only Vattier's

ancient legend, Landor found material that he could turn to his own purposes, lifting and embellishing freely to create a visionary epic that melds elements of romance, pastoral, prophecy, and tragedy.

The text exists in at least four distinct versions: 1) the anonymous edition of 1798, which is marred by numerous printing errors; 2) the edition of 1803, which adds a robust footnote commentary, along with other revisions; 3) the Latin version, *Gebirus: Poema*, that was published in November 1803, with a preface addressed to Landor's brother Robert (and likewise sundry footnotes); and 4) the version in *Gebir, Count Julian, and Other Poems*, 1831, which has very few footnotes and omits at least 75 lines of the 1803

translation and other derivative translations made from Vattier's translation remain, such as Reeve's 1785 partial translation, and the one made by John Davies in 1672. It may be noted that elements of the legend of Jubair, founder of Alexandria, are also present also in Yaqut Al-Hamawi's *Geographical Dictionary*, and in the *Khitat* of Al-Maqrizi. Al-Hamawi for instance identifies Jubair al-Mutafiki (Jubair of the cities of the plain) as the first builder of the city of Alexandria, assisted in his labor by 210,000 men. In Al-Maqrizi's *Khitat,* two separate stories seem to resemble the one preserved in Vattier's version of Murtadá. One is the story of Alexander the Great's attempts to build the city, thwarted nightly by demons of the sea, and of his eventual success. The other is that of Jiron, a founder of Alexandria who is charmed by Juriac, Princess of Egypt. This story includes several other similar elements, including the poisoning of Jiron and the nightly contest with the sea-nymph. See the following Arabic-language article by Walid Fakri for an overview of Muslim historians' writing on the founding of Alexandria: *https://manshoor.com/society/building-alexandria-muslim-myths/*. I would like to acknowledge the kind assistance of Hind Fiddah in researching the sources of this legend.

text. One revision of particular interest is the qualification of the nymph's prophecy at VI.192-93 that there shall arise from Corsica "A mortal man above mortal praise". The 1803 text carries a footnote stating that Bonaparte "might have been so", but has through abuse of monarchical authority proven the prophecy false. The 1831 text suppresses lines VI.188-201 altogether through a variant. These and a few other substantial variant passages are given in the notes to this volume. The version of *Gebir* that we reproduce here is strictly based on that of 1803, which is the version that De Quincey and Shelley read.

Between 1798 and the second edition of 1803, Landor published two other slim volumes. Both were printed in 1800, although one of them would not see publication until September 1802. *Poems from the Arabic & Persian*, released in May 1800, was a collection of pseudo-translations (or, to be more accurate, imitations) in the manner of the 14th-century Persian poet Hafez. The other volume, titled *Poetry by the Author of Gebir: and A Postscript To that Poem, with Remarks on Some Critics*, contained "The Story of Crysaor", the two longer sections of "The Phocæans", several short miscellaneous poems, and the postscript to *Gebir*.

The shortest of the three poems under discussion here, "Crysaor" has the dubious distinction of being considered either one of Landor's worst or greatest short poems.[5] The

5. Douglas Bush, Adam Roberts, and Sir Sidney Colvin characterize "Crysaor" as a powerful and affecting poem, one of Landor's best, while

titular figure of the poem, whose name means "golden sword", is borrowed from the literature of antiquity.[6] But the crux of the poem—the slaying of the hubristic autocrat Chrysaor by Neptune and the Nereïds at Jove's bidding—is absent from classical sources and is all of Landor's own invention. As such, "Crysaor" is less the rewriting of an extant classical legend than the forging of a new one. In Diodorus Siculus's telling, Chrysaor is king over all of Iberia, but in Landor's poem he is figured as the personification of Cádiz ("Gades" in the poem's spelling). Even more specifically, he would be the Isla de Léon, cut off from the Spanish mainland by the Caño de Sancti Petri, as Adam Roberts has shown in his analysis of the poem.

"The Phocæans" is likewise a loose retelling of an episode set down in the literature of antiquity. Landor found the subject for his poem while reading the historian Justin at Oxford, in particular the passages in the *Epitome of Pompeius Trogus* (43.3–4) that relate the expulsion of the Phocaeans from their homeland of Ionia in western Anatolia during the reign of Cyrus the Great. Incomplete and fragmentary, the poem relates the violence and distress that they suffer and their seafaring voyage across the Mediterranean, where they seek asylum in Tartessus and later in Gaul, at Massalia

Robert Pinsky and R. H. Super deem it a trivial failure.

6. Passages in both Hesiod's *Theogony* and the *Library* of Pseudo-Apollodorus relate how Chrysaor and Pegasus were born when Perseus beheaded Medusa. Chrysaor is the son of Medusa and Neptune.

(the site of present-day Marseilles). A detailed summary or "argument" of this notoriously obscure poem, provided by one of Landor's editors of yesteryear, is reprinted in the notes section of the present volume.

Strictly speaking, these poems were not well received. One notable exception was the favorable appreciation of Robert Southey, who was in September 1799 the first to review the anonymous *Gebir*, and who would in time become a friend and confidant of Landor. But derision somewhat prevailed, as in William Gifford's appraisal of the poem for *The Monthly Review* in 1800: "a jumble of incomprehensible trash... the most vile and despicable effusion of a mad and muddy brain that ever disgraced, I will not say the press, but the 'darkened walls' of Bedlam". Even Southey, despite his admiration of *Gebir*, found "The Phocæans" disjointed in the extreme and stated so much in *The Annual Review* in 1803. "Nothing can be imagined more obscure in its arrangement and perplexed in language than these extracts. [...] The author has continued to compress and correct till his language becomes like the contractions in old manuscripts, difficult or unintelligible; a kind of short hand which may remind him of his own conceptions, but never can explain them to another."[7]

In our time, several critics have found in Landor's abrupt and densely compressed poetic style an instance

7. "Poetry by the Author of *Gebir*," *Annual Review*, 1, 1803. pp. 663-66.

of a poet ahead of his time, displaying a proto-modernist sensibility. Robert Pinsky for one has described *Gebir* as "dazzling" in its pacing and verbal textures, akin to "motion picture speed for an audience unfamiliar with other narratives".[8] Herbert F. Tucker, in a broad survey of the British epic, writes of "The Phocæans" that "[its] inchmeal narrative advance, relieved by moments of descriptive finess, achieves an unflinching pathos peculiarly suited to his Virgian thematic of evacuation, exile, and endurance."[9] In an illuminating reading of the same poem, Adam Roberts observes that "the poem's very incompletion registers its unique force. [...] Landor's Phocæans never arrive at their destination. Instead they exist in a sort of extratemporal stasis that articulates a symbolic suspension of historical change."[10]

The harsh or generally indifferent reception of *Gebir* would eventually lead Landor to concede that the work had been a critical failure. In the preface to the 1798 edition, he had written hopefully: "If there are, now in England, ten men of taste and genius who will applaud my Poem, I declare myself content." In December 1810, he intimated his feelings about the poem's reception in a letter to Southey:

8. Pinsky, *Landor's Poetry*. University of Chicago Press, 1968, pp. 6.

9. *Epic: Britain's Heroic Muse 1790–1910*. Oxford UP, 2008, pp 83.

10. *Landor's Cleanness*. Oxford UP, 2014, pp. 79.

The *popularis aura*, though we are ashamed or unable to analyse it, is requisite for the health and growth of genius. Had *Gebir* been a worse poem, but with more admirers, and I had once filled my sails, I should have made many, and perhaps some prosperous voyages. There is almost as much vanity in disdaining the opinion of the world as in pursuing it. (Forster, *Landor. A Biography*, Vol. I, 1869, p. 178)

Here, as in the preface to "From The Phocæans", where Landor earnestly wonders "not merely whether the poetry be good, but whether it be wanted", we find a diffidence that is at odds with the author's notoriously uncompromising temperament and that is not without its pathos. We know that silence and critical censure eventually outweighed Southey's mixed praise, and as a consequence Landor changed his course: He burned his Latin version of "The Phocæans" in the fireplace, as he told Southey years later. The poetry in his next collection (*Simonidea*, 1806) resembled the poetry of 1795–1800 not at all, and his *Imaginary Conversations* were still not even a distant dream. What might Landor's works have resembled if critical opinion had lent its support to his high-flown youthful ventures? We can only imagine what strange and majestic poetry might have arisen, as we peer into the lattices of these jagged gems.

—*Jacob Siefring*

GEBIR;

A POEM:

IN SEVEN BOOKS

THE 1803 TEXT

Preface[1]

It may possibly save some trouble, and obviate some errors, if I take a cursory review of my own performance. Not that I would prevent any other from criticising it, but that I may explain at large, and state its origin and design. This Poem, the fruit of Idleness and Ignorance—for had I been a botanist or mineralogist it never had been written—was principally written in Wales. The subject was taken, or rather the shadow of the subject, from a wild and incoherent, but fanciful, Arabian Romance. On the shelf of a circulating library, I met with a Critique on the various Novels of our Country. Though the work itself had nothing remarkable in it, except indeed we reckon remarkable the pertness and petulance of female criticism, yet it presented to me, at the conclusion, the story of *Gebirus* and *Charoba*.

   Not a sentence, not a sentiment, not an image, not an idea, is borrowed from that work. I have availed myself merely of the names, and taken but few bare circumstances.

1. The former was incomplete, and was sent to the printer by mistake. Having been fairly written out, instead of another more enlarged and corrected and in several places blotted and interlined, it was as hastily put into the press—which the author, from the distance of sixteen miles and without any regular post, could not easily superintend.

I have followed no man closely; nor have I turned from my road because another stood in it; though perhaps I have momentarily, in passings caught the object that attracted him. I have chosen blank verse, because there never was a poem in rhyme that grew not tedious in a thousand lines.

In the moral are exhibited the folly, the injustice, and the punishment of Invasion, with the calamities which must ever attend the superfluous colonization of a peopled country. Gebir, the sovereign of Bœtic Spain, is urged by an oath, administered in childhood, to invade the kingdom of Egypt. He invades it. Passions, the opposite to those which he has cherished, are excited by his conference with the queen Charoba. On the other hand, her apprehensions, of which at the first alarm she had informed her attendant Dalica, from whom, as having been her nurse, she implores advice and assistance, decrease at this interview with Gebir. But women communicate their fears more willingly than their love. Dalica, all this time, intent on one sole object, and never for a moment doubting that the visible perturbation of mind proceeded, as at first, from her terrors, is determined to restore her tranquillity. She executes the plan which she had long been forming, nor discovers the love of Charoba but by the death of Gebir.

Principal Characters

Gebir, King of GADES.

Tamar, his Brother.

Charoba, Queen of EGYPT.

Dalica, her Nurse.

Myrthyr, Sister of DALICA.

Nymph, betrothed to TAMAR.

Egyptian Ambassadors.

Argument

Gebir, his habitation and habits. Alarms of *Charoba*—
imparted to *Dalica*—*Dalica's* reply. The Queen's expostu-
lation, and compliance—her interview with *Gebir*. *Gebir*
returning, meets his brother *Tamar*—*Tamar* describes his
wrestling with a *Nymph*. *Her* victory, and promise. *His*
regret and shame. *Gebir's* sympathy—his determination
to remain in *Egypt*, and to restore the city which *Sidad*,
his ancestor, had founded.

Book I

When old Silenus call'd the Satyrs home,
Satyrs then tender-hooft and ruddy-horn'd,
With Bacchus and the Nymphs, he sometimes rose
Amidst the tale or pastoral, and shew'd
The light of purest wisdom; and the God
Scatter'd with wholesome fruit the pleasant plains.

    Ye woody vales of Cambria! and ye hills
That hide in heaven your summits and your fame![1]
Your ancient songs, and breezes pure, invite
Me from my noon-tide rambles, and the force
Of high example influences my lay.

    I sing the fates of Gebir! how he dwelt
Among those mountain-caverns, which retain
His labours yet, vast halls, and flowing wells,
Nor have forgotten their old master's name[2],
Though sever'd from his people: how, incens'd

10

1. In the first edition, it was improperly printed *name*. I believe, almost every hill in that country has its descriptive name; and it often happens that the name alone is remaining of its history, and the history is apparently that of some preternatural personage. This explains the words "hide in heaven."

2. Tho' *Gibraltar* may not in strict etymology be derived from *Gebir*, nor even be correlative, yet the fiction, as it does not violate probability, is just as pardonable as the Teucro-latin name in Virgil.

By meditating on primeval wrongs,[3]
He blew his battle-horn, at which uprose
Whole nations; how, ten thousand, mightiest men,
He call'd aloud; and soon Charoba saw   20
His dark helm hover o'er the land of Nile.

    What should the damsel do? should royal knees
Bend suppliant? or defenceless hands engage
Men of gigantic force, gigantic arms?
For, 'twas reported, that nor sword sufficed,
Nor shield immense, nor coat of massive mail;
But, that upon their tow'ring heads they bore
Each a huge stone, refulgent as the stars.
This told she Dalica—then earnest cried
"If, on your bosom laying down my head,   30
I sobb'd away the sorrows of a child;
If I have always, and Heav'n knows I have,
Next to a mother's held a nurse's name,
Succour this one distress! recall those days;
Love me; though 'twere because you lov'd me then."

    But, whether confident in magic rites;
Or touch'd with sexual pride to stand implored,
Dalica smiled; then spake: "Away those fears.
Tho' stronger than the strongest of his kind,
He falls; on me devolve that charge; he falls.
Rather than fly him, stoop thou to allure,   40

3. Primeval wrongs—in not possessing, as it appears his ancestors
had, the throne of Egypt.

Nay, journey to his tents: a city stood
Upon that coast, they say, by Sidad built,
Whose father Gad built Gades; on this ground
Perhaps he sees an ample room for war.
Persuade him to restore the walls himself,
In honor of his ancestors, persuade —
But wherefor this advice? young, unespoused,
Charoba want persuasions! and a queen!"[4]

"O Dalica!" the shudd'ring maid exclaim'd,   50
"Could I encounter that fierce frightful man?
Could I speak? no, nor sigh!" "And canst thou reign?"
Cried Dalica; "yield empire, or comply."

Unfixt, though seeming fixt, her eyes down-cast,
The wonted buz and bustle of the court
From far, through sculptur'd galleries, met her ear;
Then lifting up her head, the evening sun
Pour'd a fresh splendor on her burnish'd throne, —
The fair Charoba, the young queen, complied.

But Gebir, when he heard of her approach,   60
Laid by his orbed shield, his vizor-helm,
His buckler and his corslet he laid by,
And bade that none attend him: at his side
Two faithful dogs that urge the silent course,
Shaggy, deep-chested, crouched: the crocodile,

4. Dalica, to discover the sentiments of the Queen, makes an indirect
proposal of an union with Gebir; to which she not only objects, but at
first refuses to hold any conference with him.

Crying, oft made them raise their flaccid ears,
And push their heads within their master's hand.
There was a bright'ning paleness in his face,
Such as Diana rising o'er the rocks
Shower'd on the lonely Latmian; on his brow   70
Sorrow there was, yet nought was there severe.
But when the royal damsel first he saw,
Faint, hanging on her handmaids, and her knees
Tott'ring, as from the motion of the car,
His eyes looked earnest on her; and those eyes
Shew'd, if they had not, that they might have lov'd,
For there was pity in them at that hour.
With gentle speech, and more, with gentle looks,
He sooth'd her; but, lest Pity go beyond,
And crost Ambition lose her lofty aim,   80
Bending, he kiss'd her garment, and retir'd.
He went: nor slumber'd in the sultry noon,
When viands rich, and generous wines persuade,
And slumber most refreshes; nor at night,
When heavy dews are laden with disease;
And blindness waits not there for lingering age.
Ere morning dawn'd behind him, he arrived
At those rich meadows where young Tamar fed
The royal flocks, entrusted to his care.
Now, said he to himself, will I repose   90
At least this burden on a brother's breast:
His brother stood before him: he, amaz'd,

Rear'd suddenly his head, and thus began.
"Is it thou, brother! Tamar, is it thou?
Why, standing on the valley's utmost verge,
Lookest thou on that dull and dreary shore
Where many a league Nile blackens all the sand.
And why that sadness? when I passed our sheep,
The dew-drops were not shaken off the bar,
Therefor if one be wanting 'tis untold.[5]   100

5. Of the words *"Therefor"* and *"Wherefor"* some apology is requisite for
deviating from the received orthography—tho' I could quote the authority
of Milton. It appears to me just as absurd (or even more so for the reasons
I shall give presently) to write *"therefore"* and *"wherefore"*, as it would be
to write *"whereofe"* and *"whereine."* *Fore* must ever be a long syllable; how
then is it to be managed in the words above? *"Fore,"* if it existed any where,
would be the comparison of *"first:"* but it exists only in the compound *"before."* Is it not strange to see two compound words, of which the latter half
of each is so precisely similar, so utterly different in their origin, at least in
this latter half? As *first* is a superlative which has neither a positive nor a
comparative, so another word may be remarked which is itself a positive,
and from the structure of our language, can have no regular comparative
or superlative. I mean the word *free*. We have seen, both in prose and poetry, *freer* and *freest*, and we have received them always as dissyllables.
But these vowels cannot be disjoined. *Freer* cannot exist, in obedience to
the genius of our language, nor *freest* as an adjective: tho' in the second
person singular of the verb *free*, it may be used both in prose and poetry,
observing that it can be no other than a monosyllable. Now I find myself,
tho' I came upon it unaware, on the subject of orthography, I shall add a
few words more, in which however I am not concerned. I must ask why
preceed and *exceed* are spelt differently in their termination from *recede*,
and why they are not both spelt after the manner of the latter? I would
also ask why we are so barbarously absurd as to continue the present
mode of writing *height*. I know very well the origin of it: I know that it was
in contradistinction to the passive participle or passive preterite, as we

"Yes! one is wanting, nor is that untold,"
Said Tamar, "and this dull and dreary shore
Is neither dull nor dreary at all hours."
Whereon, the tear stole silent down his cheek.
Silent, but not by Gebir unobserv'd:
Wondering he gazed awhile, and pitying spake:—
"Let me approach thee: does the morning light
Scatter this wan suffusion o'er thy brow,
This faint blue lustre under both thine eyes?"
"O, brother, is this pity or reproach,"
Cried Tamar,—"cruel if it be reproach,   110
If pity—O how vain!"
                        "Whate'er it be
That grieves thee, I will pity; thou but speak,
And I can tell thee, Tamar, pang for pang."

        "Gebir! then more than brothers are we now!
Every thing—take my hand—will I confess.
I neither feed the flock, nor watch the fold;

sometimes find it, *hight* (called). But as this preterite or participle is
out of use, why may not the substantive and adjective, hight and high,
acknowledge an unadulterated relationship? Can any thing be so absurd
as to write *simile*, and to call it an English word? It would be really an
English word, and would not *stand alone* as it does at present, if it were
written *simily*. I have thrown out these few hints that some man of learn-
ing may remove the anomalies of our language by attending to its analo-
gies. But nothing can be done without consulting Milton: his words excel
in orthography those of any other writer. If some are overloaded with
consonants, we must attribute it to the stubbornness of the Press.

How can I, lost in love? But, Gebir, why
That anger which has risen to your cheek?
Can other men? Could you? What, no reply!   120
And still more anger, and still worse conceal'd!
Are these your promises, your pity this?"
     "Tamar, I well may pity what I feel—
Mark me aright—I feel for thee—proceed—
Relate me all." "Then will I all relate,"
Said the young shepherd, gladden'd from his heart.
"'Twas evening, though not sun-set, and spring-tide[6]
Level with these green meadows, seem'd still higher;
'Twas pleasant: and I loosen'd from my neck
The pipe you gave me, and began to play.   130
O that I ne'er had learnt the tuneful art!
It always brings us enemies or love!
Well, I was playing—when above the waves
Some swimmer's head methought I saw ascend;
I, sitting still, survey'd it, with my pipe
Awkwardly held before my lips half-clos'd.
Gebir! it was a nymph! a nymph divine!
I cannot wait describing how she came,

6. It must be remembered that along the Mediterranean coasts the tides
are sensible of hardly any variation. But the coasts of Egypt are so flat,
particularly the most fertile parts, and the water so very nearly on a level
with them, that Tamar may be supposed to fancy it arising from spring-
tide. Those who have ever from a low and even country looked upon the
sea, will have observed that the sea seemed higher than the ground
where they stood.

How I was sitting, how she first assum'd
The sailor: of what happened, there remains   140
Enough to say, and too much to forget.
The sweet deceiver stept upon this bank
Before I was aware; for, with surprize
Moments fly rapid as with love itself.
Stooping to tune afresh the hoarsen'd reed,
I heard a rustling; and where that arose
My glance first lighted on her nimble feet.
Her feet resembled those long shells explored[7]
By him who to befriend his steeds' dim sight
Would blow the pungent powder in their eye.—   150
Her eyes too! O immortal Gods! her eyes
Resembled—what could they resemble—what
Ever resemble those! E'en her attire
Was not of wonted woof nor vulgar art:
Her mantle shew'd the yellow samphire-pod,
Her girdle, the dove-color'd wave serene.
"Shepherd," said she, "and will you wrestle now,
And with the sailor's hardier race engage?"[8]
I was rejoiced to hear it, and contrived

7. I make no apology for the comparison. The *Scuttle-shell*, tho' the name be inharmonious and harsh, so as not to be admissible in poetry, is of an elegant form and of a brilliant whiteness.

8. Tamar, tho' aware of her sex, affects, from the character she assumed, to consider her as a sailor, that he might with more propriety accept her challenge.

How to keep up contention;—could I fail   160
By pressing not too strongly, still to press.
"Whether a shepherd, as indeed you seem,
Or whether of the hardier race you boast,
I am not daunted, no: I will engage."
"But first," said she, "what wager will you lay?"
"A sheep," I answered, "add whate'er you will."
"I cannot," she replied, "make that return:
Our hided vessels, in their pitchy round,
Seldom, unless from rapine, hold a sheep.
But I have sinuous shells, of pearly hue   170
Within, and they that lustre have imbibed
In the sun's palace porch; where, when unyoked,
His chariot wheel stands midway in the wave.
Shake one, and it awakens; then apply
Its polished lips to your attentive ear,
And it remembers its august abodes,
And murmurs as the ocean murmurs there.
And I have others given me by the nymphs,
Of sweeter sound than any pipe you have.—
But we, by Neptune, for no pipe contend;   180
This time a sheep I win, a pipe the next."
Now came she forward, eager to engage;
But, first her dress, her bosom then, survey'd,
And heav'd it, doubting if she could deceive.
Her bosom seem'd, inclos'd in haze like heav'n,
To baffle touch; and rose forth undefined.

Above her knees she drew the robe succinct,
Above her breast, and just below her arms:
"This will preserve my breath, when tightly bound,
If struggle and equal strength should so constrain."   190
Thus, pulling hard to fasten it, she spoke,
And, rushing at me, closed. I thrill'd throughout
And seem'd to lessen and shrink up with cold.
Again, with violent impulse gushed my blood;
And hearing nought external, thus absorb'd,
I heard it, rushing through each turbid vein,
Shake my unsteady swimming sight in air.
Yet with unyielding though uncertain arms,
I clung around her neck; the vest beneath
Rustled against our slippery limbs entwined: 200
Often mine, springing with eluded force,
Started aside, and trembled, till replaced.
And when I most succeeded, as I thought,
My bosom and my throat felt so comprest
That life was almost quivering on my lips,
Yet nothing was there painful! these are signs
Of secret arts, and not of human might,
What arts I cannot tell: I only know
My eyes grew dizzy, and my strength decay'd,
I was indeed o'ercome!—with what regret,   210
And more, with what confusion, when I reached
The fold, and yielding up the sheep, she cried,
"This pays a shepherd to a conquering maid."

She smil'd, and more of pleasure than disdain
Was in her dimpled chin, and liberal lip,
And eyes that languished, lengthening,—just like love.
She went away: I, on the wicker gate
Lean'd, and could follow with my eyes alone.
The sheep she carried easy as a cloak.
But when I heard its bleating, as I did,   220
And saw, she hastening on, its hinder feet
Struggle, and from her snowy shoulder slip,
(One shoulder its poor efforts had unveil'd),
Then, all my passions mingling fell in tears!
Restless then ran I to the highest ground
To watch her; she was gone; gone down the tide;[9]
And the long moon-beam on the hard wet sand
Lay like a jaspar column half uprear'd."

    "But, Tamar! tell me, will she not return?"
"She will return: but not before the moon   230
Again is at the full; she promis'd this;
But when she promis'd I could not reply."

9. *"Gone down the tide."* By some strange blunder it was printed "gone down *to* the tide." No errors are so fatal as those which give a meaning, but give an improper one. If the *nymph* had merely gone *to* the tide, the narration of *Tamar* in all probability would not have ended—but she went *down* the tide, and consequently disappeared. Added to which, I dare not take such a liberty with a verse, even though the word should be useful and proper. The farthest that I have ventured, is, where the fastidious reader might make an elision, if he chose, in verse 190, "*If struggle* and equal strength, etc." But I believe I shall meet with no critic who will condemn this licence.

"By all the Gods! I pity thee! go on—
Fear not my anger, look not on my shame;
For, when a lover only hears of love,
He finds his folly out, and is ashamed.
Away with watchful nights, and lonely days,
Contempt of earth, and aspect up to heaven,
With contemplation, with humility,—
A tatter'd cloak that pride wears when deform'd—   240
Away with all that hides me from myself,
Parts me from others, whispers I am wise—
From our own wisdom less is to be reaped
Than from the barest folly of our friend.
Tamar! thy pastures, large and rich, afford
Flowers to thy bees, and herbage to thy sheep,
But, battened on too much, the poorest croft
Of thy poor neighbour yields what thine denies."
        They hastened to the camp; and Gebir there
—Resolved his native country to forego—   250
Ordered, that from those ruins to their right
They forthwith raise a city: Tamar heard
With wonder, though in passing 'twas half-told,
His brother's love; and sigh'd upon his own.

THE
SECOND BOOK
OF GEBIR

Argument

On the seventh morning the works are miraculously destroyed. *Gebir* exhorts his soldiers to deprecate the wrath of heaven. Proposes to *Tamar*, now the time draws near when the *Nymph* was again to meet him, that he himself should assume the brother's habit, and contend with her thus disguised. *Tamar* reluctant,—misinterprets the motive,—is satisfied,—complies. *Gebir* meets the *Nymph*— contends—conquers. Reasons suggested why the *Nymph* failed. Her astonishment—alarm—indignation—entreaty —reproach—and submission. Consoled—discovers to *Gebir* how the city is destroyed—prescribes a ceremony. He performs it. The earth opens—he descends.

Book II

The Gadite men the royal charge obey.
Now fragments, weigh'd up from th' uneven streets,
Leave the ground black beneath; again the sun
Shines into what were porches, and on steps
Once warm with frequentation—clients, friends,
All morning, satchel'd idlers all mid-day,
Lying half-up, and languid, though at games.
    Some raise the painted pavement, some on wheels
Draw slow its laminous length, some intersperse
Salt waters thro' the sordid heaps, and seize   10
The flowers and figures starting fresh to view.
Others rub hard large masses, and essay
To polish into white what they misdeem
The growing green of many trackless years.[1]
Far off, at intervals, the ax resounds
With regular strong stroke, and nearer home
Dull falls the mallet with long labor fringed.
Here, arches are discover'd, there, huge beams
Resist the hatchet, but in fresher air
Soon drop away: there lies a marble, squar'd   20
And smoothen'd; some high pillar, for its base,
Chose it, which now lies ruin'd in the dust.

1. "The growing green, etc." There was found the *Verde Antico* in
this country.

Clearing the soil at bottom, they espy
A crevice: they, intent on treasure, strive
Strenuous, and groan, to move it: one exclaims
"I hear the rusty metal grate: it moves!"
Now, overturning it, backward they start;
And stop again, and see a serpent pant,
See his throat thicken, and the crisped scales
Rise ruffled; while upon the middle fold   30
He keeps his wary head and blinking eye,
Curling more close, and crouching ere he strike.
Go mighty men, and ruin cities, go—
And be such treasure portions to your heirs.

    Six days they labor'd: on the seventh day
Returning, all their labors were destroyed.
'Twas not by mortal hand, or from their tents
'Twere visible; for these were now removed
Above, where neither noxious mist ascends,
Nor the way wearies ere the work begin.   40
There Gebir, pierced with sorrow, spake these words.

    "Ye men of Gades, armed with brazen shields;
And ye of near Tartessus, where the shore
Stoops to receive the tribute which all owe
To Bœtis, and his banks, for their attire;
Ye too whom Durius bore on level meads!
Inherent in your hearts is bravery;
For earth contains no nation where abounds
The generous horse and not the warlike man.

But neither soldier, now, nor steed, avails!   50
Nor steed nor soldier can oppose the Gods;
Nor is there aught above like Jove himself,
Nor weighs against his purpose, when once fixt,
Aught but, with supplicating knee, the Prayers.
Swifter than light are they; and every face
Though different, glows with beauty: at the throne
Of mercy, when clouds shut it from mankind,
They fall bare-bosom'd; and indignant Jove
Drops, at the soothing sweetness of their voice,
The thunder from his hand. Let us arise   60
On these high places, daily, beat our breast,
Prostrate ourselves, and deprecate his wrath."

    The people bow'd their bodies and obey'd.
Nine mornings, with white ashes on their heads,
Lamented they their toil each night o'erthrown.
And now the largest orbit of the year,[2]
Leaning o'er black Mocattam's rubied brow,[3]
Proceeded slow, majestic, and serene:
Now seem'd not further than the nearest cliff,
And crimson light struck soft the phosphor wave.   70
Then Gebir spake to Tamar in these words:—
"Tamar! I am thy elder, and thy king,

2. "The largest orbit of the year," what we call the *harvest-moon.*

3. "Black Mocattam's rubied brow." Mocattam is itself of the plural number, and is a ridge of mountains which forms the boundary of Egypt. "Rubied brow." The summits in many places are of a deeply red marble.

But am thy brother too, nor ever said,
'Give me thy secret, and become my slave';
But haste thee not away: I will myself
Await the nymph, disguised in thy attire."
Then starting from attention, Tamar cried,
"Brother! in sacred truth it cannot be!
My life is your's, my love must be my own.
O surely he who seeks a second love   80
Never felt one; or 'tis not one I feel."
But Gebir with complacent smile replied,
"Go then, fond Tamar, go in happy hour.
But ere thou goest, ponder in thy breast,
And well bethink thee, lest thou part deceiv'd,
Will she disclose to thee the mysteries
Of our calamity? and unconstrain'd?
When even her love thy strength was to disclose.[4]
My heart, indeed, is full: but witness, heaven!
My people, not my passion, fills my heart."   90
        "Then let me kiss thy garment," said the youth,
"And heaven be with thee, and on me thy grace."
        Him then the monarch thus once more addressed,
"Be of good courage: hast thou yet forgot
What chaplets languished round thy unburnt hair,
In color like some tall smooth beech's leaves
Curl'd by autumnal suns?" — How flattery

---

4. When she demanded contest before she would acknowledge her love.

Excites a pleasant, sooths a painful shame!

    "These," amid stifled blushes, Tamar said,

"Were of the flowering raspberry and vine: 100

But ah! the seasons will not wait for love,

Seek out some other now." They parted here:

And Gebir, bending through the woodlands, cull'd

The creeping vine and viscous raspberry,

Less green and less compliant than they were,

And twisted in those mossy tufts that grow

On brakes of roses, when the roses fade;

And as he pass'd along, the little hinds

That shook for bristly herds the foodful bough,

Wonder, stand still, gaze, and trip satisfied;   110

Pleas'd more if chesnut, out of prickly husk,[5]

Shot from the sandal, roll along the glade.

    And thus unnoticed went he, and untired

Stept up the acclivity; and as he stept,

And as the garlands nodded o'er his brow,

Sudden, from under a close alder, sprang

Th' expectant nymph, and seiz'd him unaware.

He stagger'd at the shock: his feet, not firm'd,

---

5. "Pleas'd more if chesnut, etc." Pleased more at such an event than at the sight of the stranger. I am afraid I have, in more than one instance, mentioned plants which are not natives of Egypt. But they may have existed there in the time of powerful kings, who would adorn their gardens and their groves with the most beautiful and rare exotics; and, in a poetical view, they may still more easily be allowed to flourish where every thing around them shoots up equally from fable.

Slipt backward from the wither'd grass short-graz'd;
But, striking out one arm, though without aim,   120
Then grasping with his other, he inclos'd
The struggler; she gain'd not one stop's retreat,
Urging with open hands against his throat
Intense; now holding in her breath constrain'd,
Now pushing with quick impulse and by starts,
Till the dust blackened upon every pore.
Nearer he drew her, and still nearer, clasp'd
Above the knees midway; and now one arm
Fell; and her other, lapsing o'er the neck
Of Gebir, swung against his back incurved,   130
The swoln veins glowing deep; and with a groan
On his broad shoulder fell her face reclined.
But ah she knew not whom that roseate face[6]
Cool'd with its breath ambrosial; for she stood
High on the bank, and often swept and broke
His chaplets mingled with her loosen'd hair.
    Whether, while Tamar tarried, came desire.
And she, grown languid, loosed the wings of love,
Which she before held proudly at her will;
And nought but Tamar in her soul, and nought   140
Where Tamar was that seem'd or fear'd deceit,
To fraud she yielded, what no force had gain'd—

6. "But ah she knew not, etc." These four verses were not inserted in the
first edition, nor were those three which follow soon after, beginning "And
nought but Tamar in her soul."

Or whether Jove, in pity to mankind,
When from his crystal fount the visual orbs
He fill'd with piercing ether, and endued
With somewhat of omnipotence—ordain'd
That never two fair forms, at once, torment
The human heart, and draw it different ways—
And thus, in prowess like a god, the chief
Subdued her strength, nor soften'd at her charms;   150
The nymph divine, the magic mistress, fail'd.
Recovering, still half resting on the turf,
She look'd up wildly, and could now descry
The kingly brow, arched lofty for command.

    "Traitor!" said she, undaunted—though amaze
Threw o'er her varying cheek the air of fear—
"Thinkest thou thus that with impunity
Thou hast forsooth deceiv'd me? dar'st thou deem
Those eyes not hateful that have seen me fall?
O heaven! soon may they close on my disgrace.   160
Merciless man; what! for one sheep estranged,
Hast thou thrown into dungeons, and of day
Amerst thy shepherd? Hast thou, while the iron
Pierced thro' his tender limbs into his soul,
By threats, by tortures, torn out that offence,
And heard him (O could I) avow his love?
Say, hast thou? cruel, hateful,—ah my fears!
I feel them true! speak, tell me, are they true?"
She, blending thus intreaty with reproach,

Bent forward, as tho' falling on her knee,   170
Whence she had hardly ris'n, and at this pause
Shed from her large dark eyes a shower of tears.
Th' Iberian King her sorrow thus consoled.
"Weep no more, heavenly damsel, weep no more,
Neither by force withheld, or choice estranged.
Thy Tamar lives, and only lives for thee.
Happy, thrice happy, you! 'Tis me alone
Whom heaven, and earth, and ocean, with one hate
Conspire on, and throughout each path pursue.
Whether in waves beneath or skies above   180
Thou hast thy habitation, 'tis from heaven,
From heaven alone, such power, such charms descend.
Then oh! discover whence that ruin comes
Each night upon our city; whence are heard
Those yells of rapture round our falling walls:
In our affliction can the Gods delight,
Or meet oblation for the Nymphs are tears?"
He spake; and indignation sunk in woe.
Which she perceiving, pride refreshed her heart,
Hope wreath'd her mouth with smiles, and she exclaim'd—
"Neither the Gods afflict you, nor the Nymphs.
Return me him who won my heart; return
Him whom my bosom pants for, as the steeds
In the sun's chariot for the western wave,
The Gods will prosper thee, and Tamar prove
How Nymphs the torments that they cause assuage.

Promise me this! indeed I think thou hast;
But 'tis so pleasing, promise it once more."
"Once more I promise," cried the gladdened king,
"By my right-hand, and by myself, I swear,   200
And ocean's Gods, and heaven's Gods I adjure,
Thou shalt be Tamar's; Tamar shall be thine."
        Then she, regarding him, long fixt, replied,—
"I have thy promise: take thou my advice.
Gebir, this land of Egypt is a land
Of incantation; demons rule these waves;
These are against thee; these thy works destroy.
Where thou hast built thy palace, and hast left
The seven pillars to remain in front,
Sacrifice there; and all these rites observe.   210
Go, but go early, ere the gladsome Hours
Strew saffron in the path of rising Morn;
Ere the bee, buzzing o'er flowers fresh disclosed,
Examine where he may the best alight
Nor scatter off the bloom; ere cold-lipt herds
Crop the pale herbage round each other's bed;
Lead seven bulls, well pastur'd and well form'd.
Their necks unblemished and their horns unring'd.
And at each pillar sacrifice thou one.
Around each base rub thrice the black'ning blood,   220
And burn the curling shavings of the hoof;
And of the forehead locks thou also burn.
The yellow galls, with equal care preserv'd,

Pour at the seventh statue from the north."
  He listen'd; and on her his eyes intent[7]
Perceiv'd her not; and now she disappear'd:
So deep he ponder'd her important words.
  And now had morn aris'n, and he perform'd
Almost the whole enjoin'd him;—he had reach'd
The seventh statue, pour'd the yellow galls,   230
The forelock from his left he had releas'd,
And burnt the curling shavings of the hoof,
Moisten'd with myrrh; when suddenly a flame
Spired from the fragrant smoke, nor sooner spired
—Down sunk the brazen fabric at his feet.
He started back, gazed—nor could aught but gaze—
And cold dread stiffen'd up his hair flower-twined:
Then with a long and tacit step, one arm
Behind, and every finger wide outspread,
He look'd and totter'd on a black abyss.   240
He thought he sometimes heard a distant voice
Breathe through the cavern's mouth, and further on
Faint murmurs now, now hollow groans reply.
Therefor suspended he his crook above,
Dropt it, and heard it rolling step by step.
He enter'd; and a mingled sound arose

7. It is not unknown that during the intensity of thought, the eye may be fixt on an object and yet not see it: something more than merely the eye, tho' open and direct, is requisite for sight—the application of mind and volition.

Like that—when shaken from some temple's roof
By zealous hand, they, and their fretted nest,—
Of birds that wintering watch in Memnon's tomb,
And tell the Halcyons when Spring first returns.   250

THE
THIRD BOOK
OF GEBIR

Argument

Gebir hears his name repeated twice. *Aröar* who had fought under his forefathers, approaches him. *Gebir* enquires with earnestness what power detains them. *Aröar* replies evasively—recapitulates the misery that would attend the disembodied Spirits having any intercourse with those on earth—then seriously addresses him, and promises, if he can endure the trial, that he shall gratify his wish. The *Gadite* kings appear—several are described. *Gebir* complains that he cannot see his father—turning to bid adieu, is clasped in his embrace. He briefly tells his son the cause of his suffering, which was the oath exacted of invading Egypt. He disappears—*Gebir* complains—reproved by *Aröar*, who reveals the laws by which these regions are governed—the flaming arch that separates the good from the wicked—once in every hundred years it suddenly starts back and discovers to each state its opposite—the contrast is exemplified in the abode of the ambitious and of the peaceful. *Aröar* teaches that those eternal fires which seem intended only for punishing the vicious, are calculated also to give verdure and pleasantness to the groves of the blest. *Gebir* asks a question on religion—the scene instantly vanishes—he rises, and visits his army.

Book III

O for the spirit of that matchless man[1]
Whom Nature led throughout her whole domain,
While he, embodied, breath'd etherial air!
    Though panting in the play-hour of my youth,
I drank of Avon, too, a dang'rous draught,
That rous'd within the fev'rish thirst of song—
Yet, never may I trespass o'er the stream
Of jealous Acheron, nor alive descend
The silent and unsearchable abodes
Of Erebus and Night; nor unchastized   10
Lead up long absent heroes into day.
When on the pausing theatre of earth
Eve's shadowy curtain falls, can any man[2]
Bring back the far-off intercepted hills,
Grasp the round rock-built turret, or arrest
The glittering spires that pierce the brow of Heav'n?
Rather, can any, with outstripping voice,
The parting Sun's gigantic strides recall?
    Twice heard was Gebir;[3] twice th' Iberian king

1. "That matchless man," Shakespear.

2. "Can any man bring back the far-off intercepted hills," or can I hope to "lead up long-absent heroes into day," so as to exhibit their perfect character by a just description of their actions?

3. "Twice heard was *Gebir*," i.e. the sound of Gebir's name.

Thought it the strong vibration of the brain   20
That struck upon his ear; but now descried
A form, a man come nearer; as he came
His unshorn hair, grown soft in these abodes,
Waved back, and scatter'd thin and hoary light.
Living, men call'd him Aröar: but no more
In celebration, or recording verse,
His name is heard, no more by Arnon's side
The well-wall'd city, which he rear'd, remains.
Gebir was now undaunted, for the brave
When they no longer doubt, no longer fear,   30
And would have spoken, but the shade began.
    "Brave son of Hesperus! no mortal hand
Has led thee hither, nor without the Gods
Penetrate thy firm feet the vast profound.
Thou knowest not that here thy fathers lie,
The race of Sidad: their's was loud acclaim
When living; but their pleasure was in war:
Triumphs and hatred followed: I myself
Bore, men imagin'd, no inglorious part;
The Gods thought otherwise![4] by whose decree   40

---

4. Let not this be considered as an imitation of the verse

    "Diis aliter visum."

There is no great merit in quoting old quotations, however apposite, and
I am of opinion that this singular passage has generally been misunder-
stood. Among all the fooleries which men have combined in their ideas of
a deity, can there be a greater than that gods and mortals have a separate

Depriv'd of life, and more, of death depriv'd,
I still hear shrieking, through the moonless night,
Their discontented and deserted shades.
Observe these horrid walls, this rueful waste!
Here some refresh the vigor of the mind
With contemplation and cold penitence:
Nor wonder, while thou hearest, that the soul
Thus purified, hereafter may ascend
Surmounting all obstruction, nor ascribe
The sentence to indulgence: each extreme   50
Has tortures for ambition; to dissolve
In everlasting languor, to resist
Its impulse, but in vain; to hear, frequent,
Nay, to take counsel from, and seek resource,
Be sooth'd by, or be scoft at by, (O Heaven!)
The vilest of mankind: to be enclosed
Within a limit, and that limit fire:
Sever'd from happiness, from eminence,
And flying, but hell bars us, from ourselves.
     Yet rather all these torments most endure   60
Than solitary pain, and sad remorse,
And tow'ring thoughts on their own breast o'erturn'd,

sense of right and wrong? Were it really the case, religious men would
become daily less zealous, and the life of the wicked be but a game of
chance; for, the virtues of the one party might not stand for virtues; nor
the vices of the other be marked for vices. There never was a doctrine
more calculated to make the generality of men despond, and to keep
them dependent on the δογματούργοι.

And piercing to the heart: such penitence,
Such contemplation, theirs! thy ancestors
Bear up against them, nor will they submit
To conquering Time th' asperities of Fate:
Yet, could they but revisit earth once more,
How gladly would they Poverty embrace,
How labour, even for their deadliest foe!
It little now avails them to have rais'd,   70
Beyond the Syrian regions, and beyond
Phœnicia, trophies, tributes, colonies:
Follow thou me: mark what it all avails."

    Him Gebir followed, and a roar confused
Rose from a river, rolling in its bed,
Not rapid—that would rouse the wretched souls—
Nor calmly—that might lull them to repose.
But with dull weary lapses it still heaved
Billows of bale, heard low, but heard afar;
For when hell's iron portals let out Night,   80
Often men start, and shiver at the sound,
And lie so silent on the restless couch
They hear their own hearts beat. Now Gebir breath'd
Another air, another sky beheld.
Twilight broods here, lull'd by no nightingale,
Nor waken'd by the shrill lark dewy-winged,
But glowing with one sullen sunless heat.
Beneath his foot nor sprouted flower nor herb,
Nor chirp'd a grasshopper; above his head

Phlegethon form'd a fiery firmament: 90
Part were sulphurous clouds involving, part
Shining like solid ribs of moulten brass:
For the fierce element which else aspires
Higher and higher, and lessens to the sky,
Below, Earth's adamantine arch rebuffed.[5]

    Gebir, though now such languor held his limbs,
Scarce aught admir'd he, yet he this admir'd;
And thus address'd him then the conscious guide.
"Beyond that river lie the happy fields.
From them fly gentle breezes, which, when drawn 100
Against yon crescent convex, but unite
Stronger with what they could not overcome.
Thus they that scatter freshness thro' the groves
And meadows of the fortunate, and fill
With liquid light the marble bowl of Earth,
And give her blooming health and sprightly force—
Their fire no more diluted, nor its darts
Blunted by passing through thick myrtle bowers,
Neither from odors rising half dissolved,
Point forward Phlegethon's eternal flame: 110
And this horizon is the spacious bow
Whence each ray reaches to the world above.
Fire rules the realms of pleasure and of pain.
Parent and element of elements,

---

5. "Earth's adamantine, etc." and repelled the flame, which had it been free would have assumed its spiral form "and lessened to the sky."

Changing, and yet unchanged, pervading heaven
Purest, and then reviewing all the stars:
All croud around him in their orbits, all
In legions for that radiant robe contend[6]
Allotted them, unseam'd and undefiled:
Then, saturate with what their nature craves, 120
Unite the grateful symphony of guests,
Take short repose, and with slow pace return.
And not the glowing oceans of the sun
Fire fills alone, and draws there smaller streams,
And dashes them on crystal cliffs of hail,
And filters through black clouds and fleecy snows—
But penetrates each cold and blue abyss
Of trackless waves, and each white glimmering gem

6. "That radiant robe" of light; "unseam'd and undefiled," unbroken in
its texture and pure in its essence. This is a personification of an oriental
cast, in which the stars are represented as crowding round their monarch,
the sun, and as receiving from him those marks of favor, which inferior
princes receive from their Sovereign. The Symphony of the stars is so
common a theme of the poets, that I shall say no more of it; their "short
repose" is in consequence of the nearest attraction to the more powerful
body. "And with slow pace return."

> Tum verò quò cuique magis curvatus eundo
> Vertitur interior devexo tramite gyrus,
> Et præceps rota vergit, eò magis impetis auctu
> *Præteriit, vacuumque fugâ eluctatur in æquor.*
> *Lentus ibi ascensu labor et cunctantior actus*
> *Objicitur, donec jam largior orbita vastum*
> *Retulerit errorem.* —

That crowns the victim's immolated brow."
    The hero pausing, Gebir then besought   130
What region held his ancestors, what clouds,
What waters, or what Gods, from his embrace.
"Young man," said Aröar, "some indeed declare
That they the spirit, when it is itself,
Have wakened on; and with fixt eyes beheld
Fixt eyes; both stricken speechless, both would speak;
Both stretch'd their kindred arms and would embrace.
That spirit, which thus struggles in its flight
To some one dearest object, with a will
Omnipotent, ne'er, after this returns: 140
Neither can mortal see departed friends,
Or they see mortal: if indeed they could,
How care would furrow up their flow'ry fields,
What asps and adders bask in every beam!
Then oft might faithful fondness from the shades
See its beloved in another's arms,
And curse immoral laws, immodest vows,
Elysium, and the vanity of soul.
She who, evading Modesty, dares take
—With sacrilegious incest most accurst—   150
The lamp of marriage from a husband's tomb,
And beckon up another, to defile
A bed new-litter'd, a mere tavern-stall,

Biting her chain, bays body; and despair[7]
Awakes the furies of insatiate lust.
Others, if worse be any, float immerst
In prisons blackly green with ropy slime,
Where toughens the brown fungus, brittle-stalk'd:
Their grosser spirits with the putrid air
Amalgamate, and, in due time, ferment   160
Seed heretofore inert; hence crawls gay-wing'd
The gadfly, hence trails forth the fulsome snake.
Living, they never own'd that Nature's face
Was lovely, never with fond awe beheld
On her parental bosom, Truth repose!"
He paus'd; then sudden, as if rous'd, renew'd.

    "But come, if ardor urges thee, and force
Suffices—mark me, Gebir, I unfold
No fable to allure thee—rise, behold
Thy ancestors!" and lo! with horrid gasp,   170
The panting flame above his head recoil'd,
And thunder thro' his heart and life-blood throb'd.
Such sound could human organs once conceive,
Cold, speechless, palsied, not the soothing voice
Of friendship, or almost of Deity,
Could raise the wretched mortal from the dust;
Beyond man's home condition they! with eyes
Intent, and voice desponding, and unheard

7. *"Bays body"* looks up with unavailing desire to the corporeal state.
The word is the strongest I could find or imagine.

By Aröar, tho' he tarried at his side.
"They know me not," cried Gebir, "O my sires,   180
Ye know me not!—They answer not, nor hear.
How distant are they still! what sad extent
Of desolation must we overcome!
Aröar, what wretch that nearest us? what wretch
Is that with eyebrows white, and slanting brow?
Listen! him yonder, who, bound down supine,
Shrinks, yelling, from that sword there, engine-hung;
He too amongst my ancestors? I hate
The despot, but the dastard I despise.
Was he our countryman?"

                            "Alas, O King!   190
Iberia bore him, but the breed accurst
Inclement winds blew blighting from north-east."
"He was a warrior, then, nor fear'd the Gods?"
"Gebir, he fear'd the Demons, not the Gods;
Tho' them, indeed, his daily face adored,
And was no warrior, yet the thousand lives
Squander'd, as stones to exercise a sling!
And the tame cruelty, and cold caprice—
Oh madness of mankind! addrest, adored!
O Gebir! what are men, or where are Gods!   200
Behold the giant next him: how his feet
Plunge flound'ring mid the marshes, yellow-flower'd.
His restless head just reaching to the rocks,
His bosom tossing with black weeds besmear'd,

How writhes he 'twixt the continent and isle!
What tyrant with more insolence e'er claim'd
Dominion? when, from th' heart of Usury
Rose more intense the pale-flamed thirst for gold?
And call'd, forsooth, *Deliverer!* False or fools!
Who prais'd the dull-ear'd miscreant, or who hoped   210
To soothe your folly and disgrace with praise.
        Hearest thou not the harp's gay simpering air.
And merriment afar! Then come, advance—
And now behold him! mark the wretch accurst,
Who sold his people to a rival king.
Self-yoked they stood, two ages unredeem'd."
"O horror! what pale visage rises there!
Speak Aröar—me, perhaps, mine eyes deceive,
Inured not, yet methinks they still descry
Such crimson haze as sometimes drowns the moon.   220
What is yon awful sight? why thus appears
That space between the purple and the crown?"
        "I will relate their stories when we reach
Our confines," said the guide, " for thou, O king,
Differing in both from all thy countrymen—
Seest not their stories, and hast seen their fates.
But while we tarry, lo again the flame
Riseth, and, murmuring hoarse, points straiter; haste!
'Tis urgent; we must on."
                            "Then, O, adieu,"
Cried Gebir, and groan'd loud; at last a tear   230

Burst from his eyes, turn'd back, and he exclaim'd
"Am I deluded? O ye powers of hell!
Suffer me — O my fathers! — am I torne" —
He spake, and would have spoken more, but flames
Enwrapt him, round and round, intense; he turn'd —
And stood held breathless in a ghost's embrace.
"Gebir, my son, desert me not, I heard
Thy calling voice, nor fate witheld me more.
One moment yet remains: enough to know
Soon will my torments, soon will thine, expire.   240
O that I e'er exacted such a vow!
When dipping in the victim's blood thy hand,
First thou withdrew'st it, looking in my face
Wondering; but when the priest my will explain'd,
Then swarest thou, repeating what he said,
How against Egypt thou wouldst raise that hand
And bruise the seed first risen from our line.
Therefor, in death what pangs have I endured!
Rackt on the fiery centre of the sun,
Twelve years I saw the ruin'd world roll round.   250
Shudder not; I have borne it; I deserved
My wretched fate; be better thine; farewell."
        "O stay, my father! stay one moment more.
Let me return thee that embrace — 'tis past —
Aröar! how could I quit it unreturn'd!
And now the gulph divides us, and the waves
Of sulphur bellow through the blue abyss.

And is he gone for ever! and I come
In vain?" Then sternly said the guide. "In vain!
Sayst thou; what wouldst thou more? alas, O prince,   260
None come for pastime here! but is it nought
To turn thy feet from evil—is it nought
Of pleasure to that shade if they are turn'd?
For this thou camest hither: he who dares
To penetrate this darkness, nor regards
The dangers of the way, shall reascend
In glory, nor the gates of hell retard
That man, nor demon's nor man's art prevail.
Once in each hundred years, and only once,
Whether by some rotation of the world,   270
Or whether will'd so by some pow'r above,
This flaming arch starts back; each realm descries
Its opposite; and Bliss from her repose
Freshens, and feels her own security."

    "Security!" cried out the Gadite king,
"And feel they not compassion?"

                            "Child of Earth,"
Calmly said Aröar at his guest's surprize,
"Some so disfigur'd by habitual crimes,
Others are so exalted, so refined,
So permëated by heaven, no trace remains   280
Graven on earth: here Justice is supreme;
Compassion can be but where passions are.
Here are discover'd those who tortured Law

To silence or to speech, as pleas'd themselves;
Here also those who boasted of their zeal,
And lov'd their country for the spoils it gave.
Hundreds, whose glitt'ring merchandize the lyre
Dazzled vain wretches, drunk with flattery,
And wafted them in softest airs to Heav'n,
Doom'd to be still deceiv'd, here still attune   290
The wonted strings and fondly woo applause;
Their wish half granted, they retain their own,
But madden at the mockry of the shades.
While on the river's other side there grow
Deep olive groves: there, other ghosts abide:
Blest indeed they; but not supremely blest.
We cannot see beyond: we cannot see
Aught but our opposite, and here are fates
How opposite to our's! here some observ'd
Religious rites, some hospitality: 300
Strangers, who from the good old men retired,
Closed the gate gently, lest from generous use
Shutting and opening of it's own accord,
It shake unsettled slumbers off their couch:
Some stopt revenge athirst for slaughter, some
Sow'd the slow olive for a race unborn.
These had no wishes; therefor none are crown'd:
But their's are tufted banks, their's umbrage, their's
Enough of sun-shine to enjoy the shade,
And breeze enough to lull them to repose."   310

Then Gebir cried, "Illustrious host, proceed.
Bring me among the wonders of a realm
Admired by all, but like a tale admired.
We take our children from their cradled sleep,
And on their fancy, from our own, impress
Etherial forms and adulating fates:
But, ere departing for such scenes ourselves,
We seize their hands, we hang upon their neck,
Our beds cling heavy round us with our tears,
Agony strives with agony. Just Gods!   320
Wherefor should wretched mortals thus believe,
Or wherefor should they hesitate to die?"
    Thus while he question'd, all his strength dissolv'd
Within him, thunder shook his troubled brain;
He started; and the cavern's mouth survey'd
Near; and beyond, his people; he arose,
And bent towards them his bewilder'd way.

THE
FOURTH BOOK
OF GEBIR

Argument

In what manner *Charoba* is affected by the report of *Gebir's* visit to the shades. Collusion of *Love* and *Terror*. Retrospect. The various ways in which *Charoba* is tormented. Universal alarm. Description of the species of patriotism that is generated under monarchy. Violence against the *Gadites* meditated. *Dalica* recommends a festival on their account. *Charoba* unsuspiciously consents—rejoices at the thought of seeing *Gebir*—hesitates—argues with herself, and is satisfied—hears tymbrels and cymbals—suspects hostility—exclaims against *Gebir*—finds that the tumult proceeds from the extravagant merriment of her own people. Description of an Egyptian holiday—of an embassy—of the *Gadites* reposing in the evening. Reception of the Egyptian elders at the Iberian tent.

Book IV

He who could pity, he who could obey,
Flatter'd both female youth and princely pride,
The same ascending from amidst the shades
Show'd Pow'r in frightful attitude: the queen
Marks the surpassing prodigy, and strives
To shake off terror in her crowded court,
And wonders why she trembles; nor suspects
How Fear and Love assume each other's form,
By birth and secret compact how allied.
Vainly, (to conscious virgins I appeal,)   10
Vainly with crouching tigers, prowling wolves,
Rocks, precipices, waves, storms, thunderbolts.
All his immense inheritance, would Fear
The simplest heart, should Love refuse, assail;
Consent—the maiden's pillowed ear imbibes
Constancy, honor, truth, fidelity,
Beauty, and ardent lips, and longing arms;
Then fades in glimmering distance half the scene,
Then her heart quails and flutters and would fly.
'Tis her beloved! not to her! ye Pow'rs!   20
What doubting maid exacts the vow? behold
Above the myrtles his protesting hand.

Such ebbs of doubt and swells of jealousy[1]
Toss the fond bosom in its hour of sleep
And float around the eyelids and sink thro'.
    Lo! mirror of delight in cloudless days!
Lo! thy reflection: 'twas when I exclaim'd
—With kisses hurried as if each foresaw
Their end, and reckon'd on our broken bonds,
And could at such a price such loss endure—   30
"O what, to faithful lovers, met at morn,
What half so pleasant as imparted fears."
How many a night serene, shall I behold
Those warm attractive orbits, close inshrined
In ether, over which Love's column rose
Marmoreal, trophied round with golden hair.
Within the valley of one lip, unseen,
Love slumber'd, one his unstrung bow impress'd.
Sweet wilderness of soul-entangling charms!
Led back by Memory, and each blissful maze   40
Retracing, me with magic power detain
Those dimpled cheeks, those temples, violet-tinged,
Those lips of nectar, and those eyes of heav'n!
    Charoba, tho' indeed she never drank[2]

1.   "Such ebbs of doubt, &c."
These three verses were not in the first edition.

2.   "Charoba, tho' indeed she never drank
            The liquid pearl, *or twined the nodding crown*, etc."
These verses allude to the history of Cleopatra. The first anecdote is well

The liquid pearl, or twined the nodding crown;
Or, when she wanted cool and calm repose,
Dream'd of the crawling asp and grated tomb,
Was wretched up to royalty! the jibe
Struck her, most piercing where love pierc'd before,
From those whose freedom centers in their tongue, 50
Handmaids, and pages sleek, and courtiers aged.
Congratulations here, there prophecies,
Here children, not repining at neglect,
While tumult thus sweeps amplest room for play;
Every-where questions, answer'd ere begun,
Every-where groups, for every-where alarm.
Thus, winter gone; nor spring, tho' near, arriv'd,
Urged slanting onward by the bickering breeze
That issues from beneath Aurora's car,
Shudder the sombrous waves; at every beam 60
More vivid, more by every breath impell'd,
Higher and higher up the fretted rocks
Their turbulent refulgence they display.
Madness, which, like the spiral element,

known: the second is less often mentioned, and perhaps less authentic.
Antony was afraid of poison. Cleopatra, to prove the injustice of his suspicions, and the ease with which the poison might be administered, if such
had been her intention, shook it, from the crown of flowers upon her head,
into a goblet of wine which she had tasted the moment before and which
she instantly presented to Antony. Before he had raised it to his lips, she
repressed him, she told him every thing, and established his confidence
for ever.

The more it seizes on, the fiercer burns,
Hurried them blindly forward, and involved
In flame the senses, and in gloom the soul.
    Determin'd to protect the country's gods,
Still asking their protection, they adjure
Each other to stand forward, and insist   70
With zeal, and trample under foot the slow;
And disregardful of the Sympathies
Divine, those Sympathies whose delicate hand
Touching the very eyeball of the heart,
Awakens it, not wounds it nor inflames.—
Blind wretches! they with desperate embrace
Hang on the pillar till the temple fall.
Oft, the grave judge alarms religious wealth,
And rouses anger under gentle words.
Woe to the wiser few, who dare to cry   80
"People! these men are not your enemies:
 Enquire their errand; and resist when wrong'd."
Together, childhood, priesthood, womanhood,
The scribes, and elders of the land, exclaim
"Seek they not hidden treasure in the tombs?
 Raising the ruins, levelling the dust,
 Who can declare whose ashes they disturb!
 Build they not fairer cities than our own,
 Extravagant enormous apertures
 For light, and portals larger, open courts,   90
 Where all ascending all are unconfin'd,

And wider streets in purer air than ours?
Temples quite plain, with equal capitals,
They build, nor bearing gods like ours imbost.
O profanation! O our ancestors!"
    Though all the vulgar hate a foreign face,
It more offends weak eyes and homely age,
Dalica most; who thus her aim pursued.
"My promise, O Charoba, I perform.
Proclaim to gods and men a festival   100
Throughout the land, and bid the strangers eat:
Their anger thus we haply may disarm."
    "O Dalica, the grateful queen replied,
Nurse of my childhood, soother of my cares,
Preventer of my wishes, of my thoughts,
O pardon youth, O pardon royalty!
If hastily to Dalica I sued,
Fear might impel me, never could distrust.
Go then, for wisdom guides thee, take my name,
Issue what most imports and best beseems,   110
And sovranty shall sanction the decree."
    And now Charoba was alone, her heart
Grew lighter; she sat down, and she arose,
She felt voluptuous tenderness, but felt
That tenderness for Dalica; she prais'd
Her kind attention, warm solicitude,
Her wisdom—for what wisdom pleas'd like her's!
She was delighted: should she not behold

Gebir? she blush'd; but she had words to speak,
She form'd them, and reform'd them, with regret   120
That there was somewhat lost with every change:
She could replace them—what would that avail—
Moved from their order they have lost their charm.
While thus she strew'd her way with softest words,
Others grew up before her, but appear'd
A plenteous, rather than perplexing, choice.
She rubb'd her palms with pleasure, heav'd a sigh,
Grew calm again, and thus her thoughts revolv'd.
     —"But he descended to the tombs! the thought
Thrills me, I must avow it, with affright.   130
And wherefor? shews he not the more belov'd
Of heaven, or how ascends he back to day.
Then, has he wrong'd me? Could he want a cause
Who has an army, and was bred to reign?
And yet no reasons against rights he urged.
He threaten'd not; proclaim'd not; I approach'd,
He hasten'd on; I spake, he listen'd; wept,
He pity'd me: he lov'd me, he obey'd;
He was a conqueror, still am I a queen."
     She thus indulged fond fancies, when the sound   140
Of tymbrels and of cymbals struck her ear,
And horns, and howlings of wild jubilee.
She fear'd; and listen'd, to confirm her fears;
One breath sufficed, and shook her refluent soul.

Smiting, with simulated smile constrain'd,[3]
Her beauteous bosom, "O perfidious man,
O cruel foe," she twice and thrice exclaim'd,
O my companions equal-aged! my throne,
My people! O how wretched to presage
This day, how tenfold wretched to endure."   150
     She ceas'd, and instantly the palace rang
With gratulation roaring into rage:
'Twas her own people. "Health to Gebir! health
To our compatriot subjects! to our queen
Health and unfaded youth ten thousand years!"
Then went the victims forward crown'd with flowers,
Crown'd were tame crocodiles, and boys white-robed
Guided their creaking crests across the stream.
In gilded barges went the female train,
And, hearing others ripple near, undrew   160
The veil of sea-green awning, if they found
Whom they desired, how pleasant was the breeze!
If not, the frightful water forced a sigh.
Sweet airs of music ruled the rowing palms;
Now rose they glistening and aslant reclined,

3. This will be unintelligible to those who have never had an opportunity
of observing the effect of the most powerful passions on the countenance;
to those in particular who have never seen extreme sorrow aroused at the
idea of ingratitude or injustice: the lips assume a strongly marked smile.
The lips are the indicators of the temper only where there is genius and
beauty, and never in brutes or brutal men, except when the whole frame
is agitated by some *evil* passion.

Now they descended, and with one consent
Plunging, seem'd swift each other to pursue,
And now to tremble wearied o'er the wave.
Beyond, and in the suburbs, might be seen
Crouds of all ages; here in triumph passed   170
Not without pomp, though raised with rude device,
The monarch and Charoba: there a throng
Shone out in sunny whiteness o'er the reeds:
Nor could luxuriant youth, or lapsing age
—Propt by the corner of the nearest street—
With aching eyes and tottering knees intent,
Loose leathery neck and wormlike lip outstretched,
Fix long the ken upon one form; so swift
Through the gay vestures fluttering on the bank,
And through the bright-eyed waters dancing round,   180
Wove they their wanton wiles, and disappear'd.

      Meanwhile, with pomp august and solemn, borne
On four white camels, tinkling plates of gold,
Heralds before, and Ethiop slaves behind,
Each with the signs of office in his hand,
Each on his brow the sacred stamp of years,
The four ambassadors of peace proceed.
Rich carpets bear they, corn and generous wine;
The Syrian olive's cheerful gifts they bear:
With stubborn goats that eye the mountain-tops   190
Askance, and riot with reluctant horn,
And steeds and stately camels in their train.

The king, who sat before his tent, descried
The dust rise redden'd from the setting sun:
Through all the plains below the Gadite men
Were resting from their labor: some surveyed
The spacious scite, ere yet obstructed, walls
Already, soon will roofs have, interposed.
Nor is the glory of no price, to take
The royal city in, as these presume.   200
Some ate their frugal viands on the steps,
Contented: some, remembering home, prefer
The cot's bare rafters o'er the high gilded dome,
And sing, for often sighs, too, end in song,
"In smiling meads how sweet the brooks repose,
To the rough ocean and red restless sands!"
But others trip along with hasty steps,
Whistling, and fix too soon on their abodes:
Haply and one among them with his spear
Measures the lintel, if so great its height   210
As will receive him with his helm unlower'd.
    But silence went throughout, e'en thoughts
        were hushed,
When to full view of navy and of camp
Now first expanded the bare-headed train.
Majestic, unpresuming, unappal'd,
Onward they marched; and neither to the right
Nor to the left, though there the city stood,
Turn'd they their sober eyes: and now they reach'd

Within a few steep paces of ascent
The lone pavilion of the Iberian king.   220
He saw them, he awaited them, he rose;
He hail'd them *"Peace be with you."* They replied
"King of the western world, be with you peace."[4]

4. Such has been precisely the eastern salutation for several hundred and even thousand years, and amongst several millions of people. The word *"peace"* is mentioned first by the person who salutes, and last by the person saluted. Perhaps the original reason is, that in nations where hostilities were common, and almost perpetual, amongst innumerable tribes, it was requisite for men to declare, immediately, explicitly, at the very first motion, the very first breath, with what intentions and sentiments they met. This true principle of natural address, and in certain instances of genuine oratory, could not escape the notice of so accurate an observer as Livy. Above the flourishes of idle eloquence, he always puts the proper word in its proper place. For example. "*Sextus Tarquinius* sum: *ferrum* in manu est: *moriere*, si emiseris vocem." I need not remark how, in addressing a woman, he first appeals to her vanity, then to her fears; first announces his rank, secondly his resolution, but the most important words invariably take the precedence. I doubt whether any other writer would have chosen a similar speech for Tarquin; more so, whether any would have been contented with so little; most of all, whether any would have done so well. Shakespear is the only one that ever knew so intimately or ever described so accurately the variations of the human character. But *Livy* is *always* great.

THE
FIFTH BOOK
OF GEBIR

Argument

Description of the city *Masar*—occupations of the inhabitants. *Dalica's* journey thither—accosted by a stranger—discovers her sister *Myrthyr*—explains to her the object of her journey—gives an account of *Charoba* from childhood—her sense and courage—enchanted by the spells of *Gebir*—reasons for thinking so—suspects that *Gebir* too is somewhat infected by the exercise of this art—how *Charoba* hates him—resolves his destruction. *Myrthyr* rejoices—takes *Dalica* home—points mysteriously to an incomplete woof. *Dalica* stands amazed. *Myrthyr* dips thrice in a poisonous dye, the garment she had shewn to *Dalica*, and delivers it as a present inevitably fatal to *Gebir*.

Book V

Once a fair city, courted then by kings,
Mistress of nations, throng'd by palaces,
Raising her head o'er destiny, her face
Glowing with pleasure, and with palms refreshed,
Now, pointed at by Wisdom or by Wealth,
Bereft of beauty, bare of ornaments,
Stood, in the wilderness of woe, Masar.
Ere far advancing, all appear'd a plain,
Treacherous and fearful mountains, far advanced.
Her glory so gone down, at human step   10
The fierce hyæna, frighted from the walls,
Bristled his rising back, his teeth unsheathed,
Drew the long growl and with slow foot retired.
Still were remaining some of ancient race,
And ancient arts were now their sole delight.
With Time's first sickle they had marked the hour
When at their incantation would the Moon
Start back, and shuddering shed blue blasted light.
The rifted rays they gather'd, and immersed
In potent portion of that wondrous wave   20
Which, hearing rescued Israel, stood erect,
And led her armies through his crystal gates.
　　　Hither—none shared her way, her counsel none—
Hied the Masarian Dalica: 'twas night,

And the still breeze fell languid on the waste.
She, tired with journey long, and ardent thoughts,
Stopt; and before the city she descried
A female form emerge above the sands:
Intent she fix'd her eyes, and on herself
Relying, with fresh vigor bent her way;   30
Nor disappear'd the woman; but exclaim'd—
One hand retaining tight her folded vest—
"Stranger! who loathest life, there lies Masar.
Begone, nor tarry longer, or, ere morn,
The cormorant, in his solitary haunt
Of insulated rock or sounding cove,
Stands on thy bleached bones, and screams for prey.
My lips can scatter them a hundred leagues,
So shrivell'd in one breath, as all the sands
We tread on, could not in as many years.   40
Wretched who die nor raise their sepulchre![1]
Therefor begone."
                    But, Dalica, unaw'd,—
Tho' in her wither'd but still firm right-hand
Held up with imprecations, hoarse and deep,
Glimmer'd her brazen sickle, and inclosed
Within its figur'd curve the fading moon—
Spake thus aloud. "By yon bright orb of Heaven,
In that most sacred moment when her beam

---

1. The Egyptians thought this the greatest calamity, from a belief that they should come to life again, at the expiration of a certain term of years.

Guided first thither by the forked shaft,
Strikes thro' the crevice of Arishtah's tower—" 50
"Sayst thou?" astonished cried the sorceress,
"Woman of outer darkness, fiend of death,
From what inhuman cave, what dire abyss,
Hast thou invisible that spell o'erheard?
What potent hand hath touched thy quicken'd corse,
What song dissolved thy cearments; who unclosed
Those faded eyes, and fill'd them from the stars?
But if with inextinguished light of life
Thou breathest, soul and body unamerst,
Then, whence that invocation; who hath dared 60
Those hallow'd words, divulging, to profane?"
Then Dalica—

        "To heaven, not earth, addrest,
Prayers for protection cannot be profane."

    Here the pale sorceress turn'd her face aside,
Wildly, and mutter'd to herself, amazed,
"I dread her who, alone, at such an hour,
Can speak so strangely; who can thus combine
The words of reason with our gifted rites;
Yet will I speak once more—If thou hast seen
The city of Charoba, hast thou marked 70
The steps of Dalica?"

                "What then?"

                        "The tongue
Of Dalica has then our rites divulged."

"Whose rites?"

     "Her sister's, mother's, and her own."
"Never."

   "How sayst thou never? one would think,
 Presumptuous, thou wert Dalica."

          "I am,
Woman, and who art thou?" with close embrace.
Clung the Masarian round her neck, and cried
"Art thou, then, not my sister? ah I fear
The golden lamps and jewels of a court
Deprive thine eyes of strength and purity: 80
O Dalica, mine watch the waning moon,
For ever patient in our mother's art,
And rest on Heaven suspended, where the founts
Of Wisdom rise, where sound the wings of Power:
Studies intense of strong and stern delight!
And thou too, Dalica, so many years
Wean'd from the bosom of thy native land,
Returnest back, and seekest true repose.
O what more pleasant than the short-breath'd sigh,
When laying down your burden at the gate,   90
And dizzy with long wandering, you embrace
The cool and quiet of a homespun bed."

   "Alas," said Dalica, "tho' all commend
This choice, and many meet with no controul,
Yet, none pursue it! Age, by Care opprest,
Feels for the couch, and drops into the grave.

The tranquil scene lies further still from Youth.
Phrenzied Ambition and desponding Love
Consume Youth's fairest flow'rs; compar'd with Youth
Age has a something something like repose.   100
Myrthyr, I seek not here a boundary
Like the horizon, which, as you advance,
Keeping its form and color, still recedes:[2]
But mind my errand, and my suit perform.

     Twelve years ago Charoba first could speak.
If her indulgent father asked her name,
She would indulge him too, and would reply
'*What? why, Charoba*'—rais'd with sweet surprize,
And proud to shine a teacher in her turn.
Shew her the graven sceptre; what its use?—   110
'Twas to beat dogs with, and to gather flies.
She thought the crown a plaything to amuse
Herself, and not the people, for she thought
Who mimick infant words might infant toys:
But while she watched grave elders look with awe
On such a bauble, she withheld her breath;
She was afraid her parents should suspect
They had caught childhood from her in a kiss;
She blushed for shame, and fear'd—for she believ'd.

2. I am not, says Dalica, the pursuer of visionary happiness; I seek not a boundary,

> "Like the horizon, which, as you advance,
> Keeping its form and color, still recedes."

Yet was not courage wanting in the child.
For I have often seen her with both hands
Shake a dry crocodile, of equal height,
And listen to the shells within the scales,
And fancy there was life, and yet apply
The jagged jaws wide open to her ear.
Past are three summers since she first beheld
The ocean: all around her earnest wait
Some exclamation of amazement wild.
She coldly said, her long-lashed eyes abased,
"Is this the mighty ocean? is this all!"
That wond'rous soul Charoba once possessed,
Capacious then as earth or heaven could hold,—
Soul discontented with capacity—
Is gone; I fear, for ever: need I say
She was enchanted by the wicked spells
Of Gebir, whom with lust of power inflamed,
The western winds have landed on our coast.
I since have watched her in each lone retreat,
Have heard her sigh, and soften out the name;
Then would she change it for Egyptian sounds
More sweet, and seem to taste them on her lips,
Then loathe them—Gebir, Gebir still return'd.
Who would repine, of reason not bereft!
For, soon the sunny stream of Youth runs down,[3]

3. When *"the stream of youth has run down,"* says Dalica, "there is
nothing to break the dull uniformity of life." Dalica lived in a court,

And not a gadfly streaks the lake beyond.
Lone in the gardens, on her gather'd vest
How gently would her languid arm recline;
How often have I seen her kiss a flower,
And on cool mosses press her glowing cheek.
Nor was the stranger free from pangs himself.   150
Whether, by spell imperfect, or, while brew'd,
The swelling herbs infected him with foam,
Oft have the shepherds met him wandering
Thro' unfrequented paths, oft overheard
Deep groans, oft started from soliloquies.
Which they believe assuredly were meant
For spirits who attended him unseen.
But when from his illuded eyes retired
That figure Fancy fondly chose to raise,
—For never had she formed so fair an one   160
Herself, till Nature shew'd an architype—
He clasped the vacant air, and stood and gazed.
Then, owning it was folly, strange to tell,
Burst into peals of laughter at his woes:
Next, when his passion had subsided, went
Where from a cistern, green and ruin'd, oozed
A little rill, soon lost; there gather'd he
Violets, and harebells of a sister bloom,
Twining complacently their tender stems

and was become an old woman: is there any thing unjust in her
reflection?

With plants of kindest pliability.   170
These for a garland woven, for a crown
He platted pithy rushes, and ere dusk
The grass was whiten'd with their roots knipt off.
These threw he, finisht, in the little rill,
And stood surveying them with steady smile;
But, such a smile as that of Gebir bids
To Comfort a defiance, to Despair
A welcome, at whatever hour she please.
Had I observ'd him I had pitied him.
I have observ'd Charoba. I have asked   180
If she loved Gebir: *'love him!'* she exclaim'd.
With such a start of terror, such a flush
Of anger, *'I love Gebir? I in love?'*
Then, looked so piteous, so impatient looked—
But burst, before I answer'd, into tears.
Then saw I, plainly saw I, 'twas not love.
For, such her natural temper, what she likes
She speaks it out, or rather, she commands.
And could Charoba say with greater ease
'Bring me a water-melon from the Nile'   190
Than, if she lov'd him, *'Bring me him I love.'*
Therefor the death of Gebir is resolv'd."

     "Resolv'd indeed," cried Myrthyr, nought surpriz'd,
"Precious mine arts! I could without remorse
Kill, tho' I hold thee dearer than the day,
E'en thee thyself, to exercise mine arts.

Look yonder; mark yon pomp of funeral;
Is this from fortune or from favoring stars?
Dalica, look thou yonder, what a train!
What weeping! O what luxury! come, haste,   200
Gather me quickly up these herbs I dropt,
And then away—hush! I must, unobserved,
From those two maiden sisters pull the spleen;
Dissemblers! how invidious they surround
The virgin's tomb, where all but virgins weep."

     "Nay, hear me first," cried Dalica, "'tis hard
To perish to attend a foreign king."[4]

     "Perish! and may not then mine eye alone
Draw out the venom drop, and yet remain
Enough? the portion cannot be perceived."   210
Away she hasten'd with it to her home:
And sprinkling thrice fresh sulphur o'er the hearth,
Took up a spindle, with malignant smile,
And pointed to a woof, nor spake a word.
'Twas a dark purple; and its dye was dread.

     Plunged in a lonely house, to her unknown,
Now Dalica first trembled; o'er the roof

---

4. It has been a custom in various countries, and was so in Egypt, on the
decease of a monarch, to kill persons that they might accompany him on
his journey. Dalica seems unwilling that Gebir should have any attendants.
She envies him even the society of the two spleenish sisters. Myrthyr sets
her at ease by assuring her that her eye alone will draw out the "venom
drop," which will not be missed, and consequently that she would not
deprive them of their lives.

Wander'd her haggard eyes—'twas some relief—
The massy stones, tho' hewn most roughly, shew'd
The hand of man had once at least been there.   220
But from this object sinking back amazed,
Her bosom lost all consciousness, and shook
As if suspended in unbounded space.
Her thus intranced the sister's voice recall'd,
"Behold it here! dyed once again, 'tis done."
Dalica stept, and felt beneath her feet
The slippery floor, with moulder'd dust bestrown.
But Myrthyr seized with bare bold-sinew'd arm
The grey cerastes, writhing from her grasp,
And twisted off his horn; nor fear'd to squeeze   230
The viscous poison from his glowing gums:
Nor wanted there the root of stunted shrub[5]
Which he lays ragged, hanging o'er the sands,
And whence the weapons of his wrath are death:
Nor the blue urchin that with clammy fin[6]
Holds down the tossing vessel for the tides.

    Together these her scient hand combined,
And more she added, dared I mention more.
Which done, with words most potent, thrice she dipt
The reeking garb, thrice waved it thro' the air: 240

5. Bruce mentions the kind of shrub, under which the cerastes burrows.

6. The Ancients supposed the echinus marinus could sink ships by fastening itself to the keel.

She ceased; and suddenly the creeping wool
Shrunk up with crisped dryness in her hands.
"Take this," she cried, "and Gebir is no more."

THE
SIXTH BOOK
OF GEBIR

Argument

Tamar's nuptials—he appears upon the waves, together with the *Nymph*, and receives with modesty and fear the congratulations of the marine deities. They and their occupations described. *Gebir* and the Egyptian ambassadors —his conduct towards them observed—they return that night. *Tamar* awakened by the *Nymph*—her fondness and delicacy—her exhortations and reflections—prognosticates danger. Courage of *Tamar*—sorrowful at hearing it will fall on *Gebir*—dissuaded from enquiry. Their voyage. Several countries described. *Ætna. Corsica*—prediction that hence shall descend "A mortal man above all mortal praise." *Tamar's* joy, however, not unmixt on beholding at a distance, and without any hopes of reaching it, his native land—his apostrophe to *Calpe*. The *Nymph's* reflections— assures him that his countrymen will have justice, and Egypt enjoy liberty and equality. The Tuscan coast. Description of the sun setting—of a waterfall under the Apennines. Triumphs of *Tamar's* descendents from the Garonne to the Rhine.

Book VI

Now to Aurora, borne by dappled steeds,
The sacred gate of orient pearl and gold,
Smitten with Lucifer's light silver wand,
Expanded slow to strains of harmony;
The waves beneath, in purpling rows, like doves
Glancing with wanton coyness tow'rd their queen,
Heav'd softly: thus the damsel's bosom heaves
When, from her sleeping lover's downy cheek,
To which so warily her own she brings
Each moment nearer, she perceives the warmth   10
(Blithe warmth!) of kisses fann'd by playful Dreams.
Ocean, and earth, and heaven, was jubilee.
For 'twas the morning, pointed out by Fate,
When an immortal maid and mortal man
Should share each other's nature, knit in bliss.
    The brave Iberians far the beach o'erspread
Ere dawn, with distant awe: none hear the mew,
None mark the curlew, flapping o'er the field:
Silence held all, and fond expectancy.
Now suddenly the conch above the sea   20
Sounds, and goes sounding thro' the woods profound.
They, where they hear the echo, turn their eyes;
But nothing see they, save a purple mist
Roll from the distant mountain down the shore.

It rolls, it sails, it settles, it dissolves.
Now shines the Nymph to human eye reveal'd.
And leads her Tamar timorous o'er the waves.
Immortals, crowding round, congratulate
The shepherd; he shrinks back, of breath bereft.
His vesture clinging closely round his limbs   30
Unfelt, while they the whole fair form admire,
He fears that he has lost it; then he fears
The wave has mov'd it; most to look he fears.
Scarce the sweet-flowing music he imbibes,
Or sees the peopled ocean: scarce he sees
Spio, with sparkling eyes, and Beroë
Demure, and young Ione, less renown'd,
Not less divine, mild-natured, Beauty form'd
Her face, her heart Fidelity; for Gods
Design'd, a mortal, too, Ione loved.   40
These were the Nymphs elected for the hour
Of Hesperus and Hymen; these had strewn
The bridal bed: these tuned afresh the shells,
Wiping the green that hoarsen'd them within:
These wove the chaplets; and at night resolved
To drive the dolphins from the wreathed door.
Gebir surveyed the concourse from the tents,
The Egyptian men around him; 'twas observ'd
By those below how wistfully he looked;
From what attention, with what earnestness   50
Now to his city, now to theirs, he waved

His hand, and held it, while they spake, outspread.
They tarried with him, and they shared the feast.
They stoop'd with trembling hand from heavy jars
The wines of Gades gurgling in the bowl,
Nor bent they homeward till the moon appear'd
To hang midway betwixt the earth and skies.
'Twas then that leaning o'er the boy beloved,
In Ocean's grot where Ocean was unheard,
"Tamar!" the Nymph said gently, "come, awake! 60
Enough to love, enough to sleep, is given.
Haste we away." This Tamar deem'd deceit,
Spoken so fondly, and he kist her lips;
Nor blushed he then, for he was then unseen.
But she arising bade the youth arise.
"What cause to fly," said Tamar; she replied
"Ask none for flight, and feign none for delay."

    "O am I then deceiv'd! or am I cast
From dreams of pleasure to eternal sleep,
And, when I cease to shudder, cease to be!" 70
She held the downcast bridegroom to her breast,
Look'd in his face and charm'd away his fears.
She said not "wherefor have I then embraced
You, a poor shepherd, or at least, a man,
Myself a Nymph, that now I should deceive?"
She said not—Tamar did, and was ashamed.
Him overcome her serious voice bespake.
"Grief favours all who bear the gift of tears!

Mild at first sight, he meets his votaries,
And casts no shadow as he comes along:[1]   80
But, after his embrace, the marble chills
The pausing foot, the closing door sounds loud,
The fiend in triumph strikes the vaulted roof,
The uplifted eye sinks from his lurid shade.
Tamar, depress thyself, and miseries
Darken and widen: yes, proud-hearted man!
The sea-bird rises as the billows rise;
Nor otherwise, when mountain floods descend,
Smiles the unsullied lotus glossy-hair'd;
Thou, claiming all things, leanest on thy claim,   90
Till overwhelm'd thro' incompliancy.
Tamar, some silent tempest gathers round!"

　　"Round whom," retorted Tamar, "thou describe
The danger, I will dare it."
　　　　　　　　　　　"Who will dare
What is unseen?"
　　　　　　　　"The man that is unblest,"
"But wherefor thou? It threatens not thyself,
 Nor me, but Gebir and the Gadite host."
"The more I know, the more a wretch am I,"
 Groan'd deep the troubled youth, "still thou proceed."
"Oh seek not destin'd evils to divine,   100

---

1. "And casts no shadow as he comes along." Those who give themselves
up to Grief, which is at first a kind of indulgence, are blind and insensible
to the consequence. That which was a humour grows a torment.

Found out at last too soon! Oh cease the search,
'Tis vain, 'tis impious, 'tis no gift of mine:
I will impart far better, will impart
What makes, when Winter comes, the Sun to rest
So soon on Ocean's bed his paler brow,
And Night to tarry so at Spring's return.
And I will tell, sometimes, the fate of men
Who loos'd from drooping neck the restless arm,
Adventurous, ere long nights had satisfied
The sweet and honest avarice of love: 110
How whirlpools have absorb'd them, storms o'er-whelm'd,
And how amidst their struggles and their prayers
The big wave blacken'd o'er the mouth supine:
Then, when my Tamar trembles at the tale,
Kissing his lips, half-open with surprize,
Glance from the gloomy story, and with glee
Light on the fairer fables of the Gods.

      Thus we may sport at leisure when we go
Where, loved by Neptune and the Naid, loved
By pensive Dryad pale, and Oread,   120
The spritely Nymph whom constant Zephyr woos,
Rhine rolls his beryl-color'd wave: than Rhine
What River from the mountains ever came
More stately! most the simple crown adorns
Of rushes, and of willows, intertwined
With here and there a flower—his lofty brow,
Shaded with vines, and mistleto, and oak,

He rears; and mystic bards his fame resound.
Or gliding opposite, th' Illyrian gulph
Will harbour us from ill." While thus she spake,   130
She toucht his eye-lashes with libant lip
And breath'd ambrosial odours; o'er his cheek
Celestial warmth suffusing: grief dispersed,
And strength and pleasure beam'd upon his brow;
Then pointed she before him: first arose
To his astonisht and delighted view
The sacred isle that shrines the queen of love.
It stood so near him, so acute each sense,
That not the symphony of lutes alone,
Or coo serene or billing strife of doves,   140
But, murmurs, whispers, nay, the very sighs
Which he himself had utter'd once, he heard.
Next, but long after, and far off, appear
The cloudlike cliffs and thousand towers of Crete:
Still further to the right, the Cyclades.
Phœbus had rais'd, and fixt them, to surround
His native Delos and aërial fane.
He saw the land of Pelops, host of Gods;
Saw the steep ridge where Corinth after stood,
Beck'ning the serious with the smiling Arts   150

Into the sunbright bay: unborn the maid[2]
That, to assure the bent-up hand unskill'd,
Look'd oft; but oft'ner fearing who might wake.
He heard the voice of rivers: he descried
Pindan Peneüs, and the slender Nymphs
That tread his banks, but fear the thundering tide:
These, and Amphrysos, and Apidanus,
And poplar-crown'd Spercheios, and, reclined
On restless rocks, Enipeus, where the winds
Scatter'd above the weeds his hoary hair.   160
Then, with Pirené, and with Panopé,
Evenus, troubled from paternal tears;
And last was Acheloüs, king of isles.
Zacynthus here, above rose Ithaca,
Like a blue bubble, floating in the bay.
Far onward, to the left, a glimm'ring light
Glanced out oblique; nor vanish'd; he inquired
Whence that arose: his consort thus replied.
"Behold the vast Eridanus! ere night
We shall again behold him, and rejoice.   170
Of noble rivers none with mightier force
Rolls his unwearied torrent to the main.

---

2. *"Unborn the maid*, etc." The story of the maid of Corinth is too celebrated
for repetition. Drawing the lines of her lover's face against the wall, I have
represented her as equally fearful of drawing them amiss, and of being
discovered by his awakening.

And now Sicanian Etna rose to view.[3]
Darkness with light more horrid she confounds,
Baffles the breath, and dims the sight, of day.
Tamar grew giddy with astonishment,
And, looking up, held fast the bridal vest.
He heard the roar above him, heard the roar
Beneath, and felt it too, as he beheld,
Hurl, from Earth's base, rocks, mountains, to the skies.   180
  Meanwhile the Nymph had fixt her eyes beyond,
As seeing somewhat; not intent on aught.
He, more amazed than ever, then exclaim'd
"Is there another flaming isle? or this
Illusion, thus past over unobserved?"
  "Look yonder," cried the Nymph, without reply,
"Look yonder!" Tamar look'd, and saw two isles
Where the waves whiten'd on the desart shore.
Then she continued. "That which intervenes[4]
Scarcely the Nymphs themselves have known from Fame:
But mark the furthest: *there* shall once arise,
From Tamar shall arise, 'tis Fate's decree,

3. This when applied to Etna will not appear too hyperbolical for poetry.
Virgil has said the like of a river. G. iii. 223.

  "Non scopuli rupesque cavæ aut objecta retardant
   Flumina, correptosque undâ torquentia *montes*."

4. "That which intervenes." Sardinia.

A mortal man above all mortal praise.[5]
Methinks already, tho' she threatens Heav'n,
Towering Trinacria to my Corsis yields."

  Tamar, who listen'd still amidst amaze,
Had never thought of progeny: he clasped
His arms with extasy around his bride,
And pleasure freshen'd her prophetic lips.
He thought too of his ancestors and home.   200
When from amidst grey ocean first he caught
The heights of Calpé, sadden'd he exclaim'd
"Rock of Iberia! fixt by Jove, and hung
With all his thunder-bearing clouds, I hail
Thy ridges, rough and cheerless! what tho' Spring
Nor kiss thy brow, nor deck it with a flower,
Yet will I hail thee, hail thy flinty couch
Where Valor and where Virtue have reposed."

  The Nymph said, sweetly smiling, "Fickle Man
Would not be happy could he not regret!   210
And I confess how, looking back, a thought
Has touched and tuned, or rather, thrill'd my heart,
Too soft for sorrow, and too strong for joy.

---

5. "A mortal man above all mortal praise." Bonaparte might have been so, and
in the beginning of his career it was augured that he would be. But unhappily
he thinks, that to produce great changes, is to perform great actions: to anni-
hilate antient freedom and to substitute new, to give republics a monarchical
government, and the provinces of monarchs a republican one; in short, to
overthrow by violence all the institutions, and to tear from the heart all the
social habits of men, has been the tenor of his politics to the present hour.

Fond foolish maid, 'twas with mine own accord,
It sooth'd me, shook me, melted, drown'd, in tears.
But weep not thou; what cause hast thou to weep.
Weep not thy country; weep not caves abhorr'd,
Dungeons and portals that exclude the day.
Gebir—tho' generous, just, humane—inhaled
Rank venom from these mansions. Rest O King   220
In Egypt thou! nor, Tamar! pant for sway.
With horrid chorus, Pain, Diseases, Death,
Stamp on the slippery pavement of the great,
And ring their sounding emptiness thro' earth.
The Hour, in vain held back by War, arrives
When Justice shall unite the Iberian binds,
And equal Egypt bid her shepherds reign.
The fairest land dry-lasht could I forego
Rather than crawl a subject; corals, pearls.
Confine me round, if Nymph can be confined,   230
'Twill not console me! Kindness prest by Power
Gives pride fresh tortures, and fresh bars constraint.
And guard me, Heaven! from that paternal care
Which beats and bruises me with iron rods,
Till I embrace them, and with tears protest
That I am happy! rather, when I sin,
Shut me from love and hide me in the deep."

    Now disappear the Liparean isles
Behind, and forward hang th' Etrurian coasts,
Verdant with privet and with juniper.   240

Now faith is plighted: piled on every hearth,
Crackle the consecrated branches, heard
Propitious, and from vases rough-embost
Thro' the light ember falls the bubbling wine.
And now the chariot of the sun descends!
The waves rush hurried from the foaming steeds:
Smoke issues from their nostrils at the gate;
Which, when they enter, with huge golden bar
Atlas and Calpé close across the main.
They reach th' unfurrow'd Appennines—all hail   250
Clime of unbounded liberty and love!—
And deep beneath their feet, a river flow'd,
Of varied view; yet each variety
So charming, that their eyes could scarce admire
The many beauties that around them throng'd,
Successive as the wave: aspiring elms
O'er the wide water cast a mingled shade
Of tendrils green and grapes of rosy hue.
Among the branches thousand birds appear'd
To raise their little throats, with trilling song   260
Unwearied, but alas their trilling song,
Fast as it flow'd, the roaring torrent drown'd.
Some, unacquainted with the scene, unmoved
By love of tuneful mate, on timid wing
Fly from the eternal thunder of the waves;
But these, content with humid woods, that yield
The choicest moss to warm their callow young,

Brood over them, nor shudder at the damp
That falls for ever round each circled nest.
Here craggy rocks arise; the stream recoils 270
Struggling; but, hurried to the vast abyss
Abruptly, reascends in gloomy rain;
Bespangling in its way the scatter'd herbs
That cling around each lofty precipice,
Of wintry blasts regardless, and the reeds
Which never shall amuse with shrill essay
The valley or the grove, and tender flowers
On virgin bosom never to repose.
But all around them dart the wandering rays
In myriads, and amid the fresh festoons 280
Of pensile vines a hundred arches bend;
Rais'd by the hand of Phœbus and of Jove,
The seats of Iris. — Rise, Iberian Man!
Rise, maid of Ocean! I myself will rise.
Vigorous with youth, with soaring soul endued,
I feel not earth beneath me — lo I snatch
The sunbeam, scorn the thunder, climb the skies
What force have you inform'd me with! what sight,
Piercing thro' darkness and futurity.

Yonder, where, sailing slow, the clouds retire, 290
How grand a prospect opens! Alps o'er Alps

Tower, to survey the triumphs that proceed.[6]
There, while Garumna[7] dances in the gloom
Of larches, mid her Naids, or reclined
Leans on a broom-clad bank to watch the sports
Of some far-distant chamois silken-hair'd,
The chaste Pyrené, drying up her tears,
Finds, with your children, refuge: yonder, Rhine
Lays his imperial sceptre at their feet.

6. The following verses, which in themselves are not perhaps worse than any others in the poem, were at first omitted; that too much might not be said on one subject, and that the just proportions of the book, might be preserved.

> "If Glory call ye, turn to Mercy's side,
> Ye sons of Gaul, for Glory waits ye there.
> Pale Monarchy flies past! her Asian vase,
> Graven with tigers linked before her car,
> And riot Loves, and Satyrs, crown'd with flowers,
> Round which whole nations reel'd away from Truth—
> Flaw'd with the spear, and on the sands reverst,
> Spills the slow poison that consumed the brave.
> Now, Youth exult! now, harass'd Age, repose!
> Yours are the rural Sports, unchill'd by Fear,
> Yours, Plenty, Peace, and Liberty, that loves
> The household gods, and late unsheaths the sword.
> Round every cottage, and thro' every wild,
> For you the vine her purple wreath suspends,
> The glaucous olive bears the cold for you.
> Lo! while Garumna dances in the shade, etc."

7. "Garumna," the river Garonne, which rises in the Pyrenean mountains.

What hoary form so vigorous vast bends there? 300
Time,—Time himself throws off his motly garb
Figur'd with monstrous men and monstrous gods,
And in pure vesture enters their pure fanes,
A proud partaker of their festivals.
Captivity led captive, War o'erthrown,
They shall, o'er Europe, shall o'er Earth extend
Empire that seas alone and skies confine,[8]
And glory that shall strike the crystal stars.

8. "Empire that seas alone and skies confine." The empire of justice and equality. Great hopes were raised from the French revolution, but every good man is disappointed. God forbid that we should ever be impelled to use their means of amelioration, or that our arms should be attended by success, like theirs,—internal and external subjugation.

THE
SEVENTH BOOK
OF GEBIR

Argument

Against colonization in peopled countries. All nature dissuades from whatever is hostile to equality. The day, according to expectation, of *Charoba's* marriage with *Gebir*. The games of the Tartessians, Gadites, Nebrissans, etc. Sensations of *Gebir*—of Charoba. Description of her bath. Preparations. Ardor of the people. She sets out. *Gebir* meets her. Observation by one of her handmaids. The procession. They mount their thrones. *Dalica* appears—throws perfumes over the head and feet of *Gebir*—draws over his shoulders the deadly garment. *Charoba*, who observes, but misinterprets the change in his countenance, with an emotion of tenderness and fear, expects the declaration of his love. He descends from his throne. Astonishment of the Iberians. Horror of *Charoba*—her grief—her love—repeats his name—embraces him in the agonies of despair—calls earth and heaven to attest her innocence—laments most passionately that wretchedness like her's must seem infinitely too great for any thing but guilt—implores instant death—appeals to *Dalica*—acquits *her* of any evil intentions—but accuses the *demons* of tainting the deadly robe—apostrophe to her parents, particularly to her mother—to *Gebir*. He recovers to perceive her sorrows, is consoled, and dies.

Book VII

What mortal first, by adverse fate assail'd,
Trampled by tyranny, or scoft by scorn,
Stung by remorse, or wrung by poverty,
Bade, with fond sigh, his native land farewel?
Wretched! but tenfold wretched, who resolv'd
Against the waves to plunge th' expatriate keel,
Deep with the richest harvest of his land!
     Driven with that weak blast which Winter leaves,[1]
Closing his palace-gates on Caucasus,
Oft hath a berry risen forth a shade: 10
From the same parent plant, another lies
Deaf to the daily call of weary hind—
Zephyrs pass by, and laugh at his distress.
By every lake's and every river's side[2]
The Nymphs and Naids teach Equality:
In voices gently querulous they ask
"Who would with aching head and toiling arms

1. Those who have left their country from a sense of injustice or from indifference, have often flourished; while those whom the mother country has sent out with great care and expence, have utterly deceived her expectations.

2. Here are twenty verses which were not in the first edition. They describe the equality which nature teaches, the absurdity of colonizing a country which is peopled, and the superior advantage of cultivating those which remain unoccupied.

Bear the full pitcher to the stream far off?
Who would, of power intent on high emprize,
Deem less the praise to fill the vacant gulph   20
Than raise Charybdis upon Etna's brow?"
Amidst her darkest caverns most retired,
Nature calls forth her filial Elements
To close around and crush that monster *Void*.—
Fire, springing fierce from his resplendent throne,
And Water, dashing the devoted wretch
Woundless and whole, with iron-colour'd mace,
Or whirling headlong in his war-belt's fold.
Mark well the lesson, man! and spare thy kind.
Go, from their midnight darkness wake the woods,   30
Woo the lone forest in her last retreat—
Many still bend their beauteous heads unblest
And sigh aloud for elemental man.
Thro' palaces and porches, evil eyes
Light upon ev'n the wretched, who have fled
The house of bondage, or the house of birth:
Suspicions, murmurs, treacheries, taunts, retorts,
Attend the brighter banners that invade;
And the first horn of hunter, pale with want,
Sounds to the chase; the second to the war.   40

     The long awaited day at last arrived,
When, linkt together by the seven-arm'd Nile,
Egypt with proud Iberia should unite.
Here the Tartessian, there the Gadite tents

Rang with impatient pleasure: here engaged
Woody Nebrissa's quiver-bearing crew,
Contending warm with amicable skill:
While they of Durius raced along the beach,
And scatter'd mud and jeers on those behind.
The strength of Bœtis, too, removed the helm,   50
And stript the corslet off, and staunched the foot
Against the mossy maple, while they tore
Their quivering lances from the hissing wound.
Others pushed forth the prows of their compeers;
And the wave, parted by the pouncing beak,
Swells up the sides, and closes far astern:
The silent oars now dip their level wings,
And weary with strong stroke the whitening wave.
Others, afraid of tardiness, return.
Now, entering the still harbour, every surge   60
Runs with a louder murmur up their keel,
And the slack cordage rattles round the mast.
Sleepless, with pleasure and expiring fears,
Had Gebir risen ere the break of dawn,
And o'er the plains appointed for the feast
Hurried with ardent step: the swains admired
What could so transversely sweep off the dew,
For never long one path had Gebir trod,
Nor long, unheeding man, one pace preserved.
Not thus Charoba. She despair'd the day.   70
The day was present: true: yet she despair'd.

In the too tender and once tortured heart
Doubts gather strength from habit, like disease;
Fears, like the needle verging to the pole,
Tremble and tremble into certainty.
How often, when her maids with merry voice
Call'd her, and told the sleepless queen 'twas morn,
How often would she feign some fresh delay,
And tell them (tho' they saw) that she arose.[3]
Next to her chamber, closed by cedar doors,   80
A bath, of purest marble, purest wave,
On its fair surface bore its pavement high.
Arabian gold inclosed the crystal roof,
With fluttering boys adorn'd and girls unrobed,
These, when you touch the quiet water, start
From their aërial sunny arch, and pant
Entangled midst each other's flowery wreaths,
And each pursuing is in turn pursued.
        Here came at last, as ever wont at morn,
Charoba: long she linger'd at the brink,   90
Often she sighed, and, naked as she was,
Sat down, and leaning on the couch's edge,
On the soft inward pillow of her arm
Rested her burning cheek: she moved her eyes;

3. "Tho' they saw." If this were not taken parenthetically, and read so, it would convey a double sense. Charoba told the attendants that she was rising, "tho' they saw"—tho' they were in the apartment, and could perceive that there were no preparations for that purpose.

She blush'd; and blushing plung'd into the wave.

      Now brazen chariots thunder thro' each street,
And neighing steeds paw proudly from delay.
While o'er the palace breathes the dulcimer,
Lute, and aspiring harp, and lisping reed;
Loud rush the trumpets, bursting thro' the throng,   100
And urge the high-shoulder'd vulgar; now are heard
Curses and quarrels and constricted blows,
Threats and defiance and suburban war.
Hark! the reiterated clangor sounds!
Now murmurs, like the sea, or like the storm,
Or like the flames on forests, move and mount
From rank to rank, and loud and louder roll,
Till all the people is one vast applause.
Yes, 'tis herself—Charoba—now the strife!
To see again a form so often seen.   110
Feel they some partial pang, some secret void,
Some doubt of feasting those fond eyes again?
Panting imbibe they that refreshing sight[4]
To reproduce in hour of bitterness?
She goes; the king awaits her from the camp.
Him she descried; and trembled ere he reached

4. "Panting imbibe they that refreshing sight
    To reproduce in hour of bitterness?"

This metaphor is taken from the country. It alludes to the camel, which is said to be able to refresh itself with the water which it has imbibed and secreted many days.

Her car; but shudder'd paler at his voice.
So the pale silver at the festive board
Grows paler fill'd afresh and dew'd with wine;
So seems the tenderest herbage of the spring   120
To whiten, bending from a balmy gale.
The beauteous queen alighting he received,
And sighed to loose her from his arms; she hung
A little longer on them thro' her fears,
Her maidens followed her: and one that watch'd,
One that had call'd her in the morn, observ'd
How virgin passion with unfuel'd flame
Burns into whiteness; while the blushing cheek
Imagination heats and Shame imbues.

      Between both nations, drawn in ranks, they pass.   130
The priests, with linen ephods, linen robes,
Attend their steps, some follow, some precede,
Where, cloath'd with purple intertwined with gold,
Two lofty thrones commanded land and main.
Behind and near them, numerous were the tents
As freckled clouds o'erfloat our vernal skies,
Numerous as wander in warm moonlight nights,
Along Meander's or Cäyster's marsh,
Swans, pliant-neckt, and village storks, revered.
Throughout each nation moved the hum confused,   140
Like that from myriad wings, o'er Scythian cups
Of frothy milk, concreted soon with blood.
Throughout the fields the savory smoke ascends,

And boughs and branches shade the hides unbroached.
Some roll the flowery turf to form a seat,
And others press the helmet—now resounds
The signal!—queen and monarch mount the thrones.
The brazen clarion hoarsens: many leagues
Above them, many to the south, the hern
Rising with hurried croak and throat outstretched,   150
Plows up the silvering surface of her plain.
  Tottering, with age's zeal, and mischief's haste,
Now was discover'd Dalica: she reached
The throne: she lean'd against the pedestal;
And now ascending stood before the king.
Prayers for his health and safety she prefer'd,
And o'er his head and o'er his feet she threw
Myrrh, nard, and cassia, from three golden urns.
His robe of native woof she next removed,
And round his shoulders drew the garb accurst,   160
And bow'd her head, and parted: soon the queen
Saw the blood mantle in his manly cheeks,
And fear'd, and fault'ring sought her lost replies,
And blest the silence that she wished were broke.
Alas, unconscious maiden! night shall close,
And love, and sovereignty, and life dissolve,
And Egypt be one desert drench'd in blood.
  When thunder overhangs the fountain's head,
Losing their wonted freshness, every stream
Grows turbid, grows with sickly warmth suffused: 170

Thus were the brave Iberians, when they saw
The king of nations from his throne descend.
Scarcely, with pace uneven, knees unnerved,
Reach'd he the waters: in his troubled ear
They sounded murmuring drearily; they rose
Wild, in strange colours, to his parching eyes:
They seem'd to rush around him, seem'd to lift
From the receding earth his helpless feet.
He fell—Charoba shriek'd aloud—she ran—
Frantic with fears and fondness, wild with woe,   180
Nothing but Gebir dying she beheld.
The turban that betray'd its golden charge
Within, the veil that down her shoulders hung,
All fallen at her feet! the furthest wave
Creeping with silent progress up the sand,
Glided thro' all, and rais'd their hollow folds.
In vain they bore him to the sea, in vain
Rubb'd they his temples with the briny warmth.
He struggled from them, strong with agony,
He rose half up; he fell again; he cried   190
"Charoba! O Charoba!" She embraced
His neck, and raising on her knee one arm,
Sighed when it moved not, when it fell she shrieked.
And clasping loud both hands above her head,
She call'd on Gebir, call'd on earth, on heaven.

"Who will believe me; what shall I protest;
How innocent, thus wretched?[5] God of Gods,
Strike me—who most offend thee most defy—
Charoba most offends thee—strike me, hurl
From this accursed land, this faithless throne.   200
O Dalica! see here the royal feast!
See here the gorgeous robe! you little thought
How have the demons dyed that robe with death.
Where are ye, dear fond parents! when ye heard
My feet in childhood pat the palace floor,
Ye started forth, and kist away surprize—
Will ye now meet me! how, and where, and when?
And must I fill your bosom with my tears,
And, what I never have done, with your own!
Why have the Gods thus punish'd me? what harm   210
Have ever I done them? have I profaned
Their temples, ask'd too little, or too much?
Proud if they granted, griev'd if they withheld?
O mother! stand between your child and them!
Appease them, soothe them, soften their revenge,
Melt them to pity with maternal tears.
Alas, but if you cannot!—they themselves
Will then want pity rather than your child.

5. "How innocent, thus wretched?" How shall I appear innocent in the
eyes of mankind, when the Gods have afflicted me with so grievous a
calamity? She has no suspicion that Dalica was conscious of the effect
which the robe had produced.

O Gebir! best of monarchs, best of men,
What realm hath ever thy firm even hand   220
Or lost by feebleness, or held by force!
Behold, thy cares and perils how repaid!
Behold the festive day, the nuptial hour!
Me miserable, desolate, undone!"

       Thus raved Charoba: horror, grief, amaze,
Pervaded all the host: all eyes were fixt:
All stricken motionless and mute—the feast
Was like the feast of Cepheus,[6] when the sword
Of Phineus, white with wonder, shook restrain'd,
And the hilt rattled in his marble hand.   230
She heard not, saw not; every sense was gone;
One passion banish'd all; dominion, praise,
The world itself was nothing—Senseless man—
What would thy fancy figure now from worlds?
There is no world to those that grieve and love.
She hung upon his bosom, prest his lips,
Breath'd, and would feign it his that she resorbed.
She chafed the feathery softness of his veins,
That swell'd out black, like tendrils round their vase
After libation: lo! he moves! he groans!   240
He seems to struggle from the grasp of death.
Charoba shriek'd, and fell away; her hand
Still clasping his, a sudden blush o'erspread

---

6. "The feast of Cepheus." This story is told at large in the *Metamorphoses* of Ovid. Phineus was turned into marble by the Gorgon shield.

Her pallid humid cheek, and disappear'd.
'Twas not the blush of shame—what shame has woe?—
'Twas not the genuine ray of hope; it flashed
With shuddering glimmer thro' unscatter'd clouds;
It flash'd from passions rapidly opposed.

      Never so eager, when the world was waves,
Stood the less daughter of the ark, and tried   250
(Innocent this temptation!) to recall
With folded vest, and casting arm, the dove:
Never so fearful, when amidst the vines
Rattled the hail, and when the light of heaven
Closed, since the wreck of Nature, first eclipsed—
As she was eager for his life's return,
As she was fearful how his groans might end.
They ended:—cold and languid calm succeeds.
His eyes have lost their lustre; but his voice
Is not unheard, tho' short: he spake these words.   260

      "And weepest thou, Charoba! shedding tears
More precious than the jewels that surround
The neck of kings entomb'd!—then weep, fair queen,
At once thy pity and my pangs assuage.
Ah! what is grandeur—glory—they are past!
When nothing else, nor life itself remains,
Still the fond mourner may be call'd our own.
Should I complain of Fortune? how she errs,
Scattering her bounty upon barren ground,
Slow to allay the lingering thirst of Toil?   270

Fortune, 'tis true, may err, may hesitate;
Death follows close, nor hesitates nor errs.
I feel the stroke! I die!" He would extend
His dying arm; it fell upon his breast.
Cold sweat and shivering ran o'er every limb.
His eyes grew stiff; he struggled and expired.

CRYSAOR

Advertisement to The Story of Crysaor

Hardly any thing remains that made ancient Iberia classic land. We have little more than the titles of fables—than portals, as it were, covered over with gold and gorgeous figures, that shew us what once must have been the magnificence of the whole interior edifice. Lucan has wandered over Numidia, and Virgil too at the conclusion of his Georgics, has left the indelible mark of his footstep near the celebrated Pharos of Egypt. But, in general, the poets of Greece and Italy were afraid of moving far from the latest habitations of their tutelar gods and heroes. I am fond of walking by myself; but others, who have gone before me, may have planted trees, or opened vistas, and rendered my walks more amusing. I had begun to write a poem connected in some degree with the early history of Spain; but doubtful whether I should ever continue it, and grown every hour more indifferent, I often sat down and diverted my attention with the remotest views I could find. The present is a sketch.

The Story of Crysaor

Come, I beseech ye, Muses! who, retired
Deep in the shady glens by Helicon,
Yet know the realms of ocean, know the laws
Of his wide empire, and throughout his court
Know every Nymph, and call them each by name
Who from your sacred mountain see afar
O'er earth and heaven, and hear and memorize
The crimes of men and counsels of the Gods;
Sing of those crimes and of those counsels, sing
Of Gades sever'd from the fruitful main;   10
And what befel, and from what mighty hand,
Crysäör, sovereign of the golden sword.
    'Twas when the high Olympus shook with fear,
Lest all his temples, all his groves, be crushed
By Pelion piled on Ossa: but the sire
Of mortals and immortals waved his arm
Around, and all below was wild dismay:
Again—'twas agony: again—'twas peace.
Crysäör still in Gades tarrying,
Hurl'd into ether, tinging, as it flew,   20
With sudden fire the clouds round Saturn's throne,
No pine surrender'd by retreating Pan,
Nor ash, nor poplar pale; but swoln with pride
Stood towering from the citadel; his spear

One hand was rested on, and one with rage
Shut hard, and firmly fixt against his side;
His frowning visage, flusht with insolence,
Rais'd up oblique to heaven. "O thou," he cried,
"Whom nations kneel to, not whom nations know,
Hear me, and answer, if indeed thou can'st,   30
The last appeal I deign thee or allow.
Tell me, and quickly, why should I adore,
Adored myself by millions? why invoke,
Invoked with all thy attributes? men wrong
By their prostrations, prayers, and sacrifice,
Either the gods, their rulers, or themselves:
But flame and thunder fright them from the *Gods*,
Themselves they cannot, dare not—they are *ours*,
Us—dare they, can they, *us*? but triumph, Jove!
Man for one moment hath engaged his lord,   40
Henceforth let merchants value him, not kings.[1]

1. *Henceforth let merchants value him, not kings*. It may seem contradictory
that merchants should be mentioned here, when in verse 166 it is
expressly said

> "Not ever had the veil-hung pine outspread
> O'er Tethys then *her wandering leafless shade*."

But *foreign* merchants are not necessarily understood. Those who cannot
disengage the idea of slave-merchants from the Europeans in Guinea,
may still recollect that there were some native ones in that country an-
tecedent to our own, and that the princes themselves sold their prisoners
to any of the neighbouring tribes. It does not require the practice of navi-
gation to make or sell slaves. The petty princes of Hesse and Hanover
have within our own memory committed this outrage on humanity, like

No! lower thy sceptre, and hear Atrobal,
And judge aright to whom men sacrifice.
My children, said the sage and pious priest,
Mark there the altar! tho' the fumes aspire
Twelve cubits ere a nostril they regale,
'Tis myrrh for Titans, 'tis but air for Gods.
Time changes, Nature changes, I am changed!
Fronting the furious lustre of the sun,
I yielded to his piercing swift-shot beams   50
Only when quite meridian, then abased
These orbits to the ground, and there surveyed
My shadow — strange and horrid to relate!

their brethren the petty princes of Negroland: with this one difference —
that the former calculated how much more valuable the cargo would be
to the taskmaster if employed in the ruin and slaughter of those whom he
had rendered his enemies, than in merely tilling the earth like the African,
and therefor set a greater price on the service of a few years, because
the service was *summary*, than their brethren in Negroland usually do on
a gentler and less degrading one for life.

This poem describes a period when the insolence of tyranny and
the sufferings of mankind were at the utmost. They could not be so without slavery; and slavery could not generally exist without some sort of
barter. Merchants then were necessary. It appears that Crysaor, wicked
as he is represented, had no personal share in it's propagation. He encouraged it. But, a Sovereign who is powerful enough, either by the fears
or affection of his people, to abolish from amongst them this inhuman
traffic, and who makes not one effort, uses not one persuasion, for the
purpose, deserves the execration which followed, and the punishment
which overtook Crysaor. Every man, instead of waiting with awe for some
preternatural blow, should think *himself* a particle of those elements
which Providence has decreed to crush so abominable monster.

My very shadow almost disappeared!
Restore it, or by earth and hell I swear
With blood enough will I refascinate
The cursed incantation: thou restore,
And largely; or my brethren, all combined,
Shall rouse thee from thy lethargies, and drive
Far from thy cloud-soft pillow, minion-prest,   60
Those leering lassitudes that follow Love."

    The smile of disappointment and disdain
Sat sallow on his pausing lip half-closed;
But, neither headlong importunity,
Nor gibing threat of reed-propt insolence,
Let loose the blast of vengeance: heaven shone bright,
Still, and Crysäör spurn'd the prostrate land.
But the triumphant Thunderer, now mankind
(Criminal mostly for enduring crimes—)
Provoked his indignation, thus besought   70
His trident-sceptred brother, triton-home.
"O Neptune! cease henceforward to repine.
They are not cruel, no—the destinies
Intent upon their loom, unoccupied
With aught beyond it's moody murmuring sound,
Will neither see thee weep nor hear thee sigh:
And wherefor weep, O Neptune, wherefor sigh!
Ambition? 'tis unworthy of a God,
Unworthy of a brother! I am Jove,

Thou, Neptune,—happier in uncitied realms,   80
In coral hall or grotto samphire-ciel'd,
Amid the song of Nymphs and ring of shells,
Thou smoothest at thy will the pliant wave
Or liftest it to heaven.—I also can
Whatever best beseems me, nor for aid
Unless I loved thee, Neptune, would I call.
Tho' absent, thou hast heard, and hast beheld,
The profanation of that monsterous race,
That race of earth-born giants—one survives—
The rapid-footed Rhodan, mountain-rear'd,   90
Beheld the rest defeated; still remain
Scatter'd throughout interminable fields,
Sandy and sultry, and each hopeless path
Choaked up with crawling briars and bristling thorns,
The flinty trophies of their foul disgrace.
Crysäör, Sovereign of the golden sword,
Still hails as brethren men of stouter heart,
But, wise confederate, shuns Phlegrœan fields.
No warrior he, yet who so fond of war,
Unfeeling, scarce ferocious; flattery's dupe   100
He fancies that the gods themselves are his;
Impious, but most in prayer:—now re-assert
Thy friendship, raise thy trident, strike the rocks,
Sever him from mankind." Then thus replied
The Nymph-surrounded monarch of the main.

"Empire bemoan I not, however shared,
Nor Fortune frail, nor stubborn Fate, accuse:
No!—mortals I bemoan! when Avarice,
Plowing these fruitless furrows, shall awake
The basking Demons, and the dormant Crimes,   110
Horrible, strong, resistless, and transform
Meekness to Madness, Patience to Despair.
What is Ambition? What but Avarice?
But Avarice in richer guize arrayed,
Stalking erect, loud-spoken, lion-mien'd,
Her brow uncrost by care, but deeply markt,
And darting downwards 'twixt her eyes hard-lasht
The wrinkle of command.—could ever I
So foul a fiend, so fondly too, caress?
Judge me not harshly, judge me by my deeds."   120

Tho' seated then on Africs further coast,
Yet sudden, at his voice, so long unheard—
For he had grieved, and treasured up his grief—
With short kind greeting, meet from every side
The Triton herds, and warm with melody
The azure concave of their curling shells.
Swift as an arrow, as the wind, as light,
He glided thro' the deep, and now, arrived,
Lept from his pearly beryl-studded car.
Earth trembled—the retreating tide, black-brow'd,   130
Gather'd new strength, and rushing on, assail'd

The promontory's base: but when the God
Himself, resistless Neptune, struck one blow,
Rent were the rocks asunder, and the sky
Was darkened with their fragments ere they fell.
Lygea vocal, Zantho yellow-hair'd,
Spio with sparkling eyes, and Beroë
Demure, and sweet Iöné, youngest-born,
Of mortal race, but grown divine by song—
Had you seen playing round her placid neck   140
The sunny circles, braidless and unbound,—
O! who had call'd them boders of a storm!
These, and the many sister Nereïds,
Forgetful of their lays and of their loves,
All, unsuspicious of the dread intent,
Stop suddenly their gambols, and with shrieks
Of terror plunge amid the closing wave:
Still, just above, one moment more, appear
Their darken'd tresses floating in the foam.

     Thrown prostrate on the earth, the Sacrilege   150
Rais'd up his head astounded, and accurs'd
The stars, the destinies, the gods—his breast
Panted from consternation, and dismay,
And pride untoward, on himself o'erthrown.
From his distended nostrils issued gore,
At intervals, with which his wiry locks,
Huge arms, and bulky bosom, shone beslimed:
And thrice he call'd his brethren, with a voice

More dismal than the blasts from Phlegethon
Below, that urge along ten thousand ghosts   160
Wafted loud-wailing o'er the firey tide.
But answer heard he none — the men of might
Who gather'd round him formerly, the men
Whom frozen at a frown, a smile revived,
Were far — enormous mountains interposed,
Nor ever had the veil-hung pine out-spread
O'er Tethys then her wandering leafless shade:
Nor could he longer under wintry stars
Suspend the watery journey, nor repose
Whole nights on Ocean's billowy restless bed;   170
No longer, bulging thro' the tempest, rose
That bulky bosom; nor those oarlike hands,
Trusted ere mortal's keenest ken conceived
The bluest shore — threw back opposing tides.
Shrunken mid brutal hair his violent veins
Subsided, yet were hideous to behold
As dragons panting in the noontide brake.
At last, absorbing deep the breath of heaven,
And stifling all within his deadly grasp,
Struggling, and tearing up the glebe, to turn;   180
And from a throat that, as it throb'd and rose,
Seem'd shaking ponderous links of dusky iron,
Uttering one anguish-forced indignant groan,
Fired with infernal rage, the spirit flew.

Nations of fair Hesperia! lo o'erthrown
Your peace-embracing war-inciting king!
Ah! thrice twelve years, and longer, ye endured
Without one effort to rise higher, one hope
That heaven would wing the secret shaft aright,
The abomination!—hence 'twas Jove's command   190
That, many hundred, many thousand, more,
Freed from one despot, still from one unfreed,
Ye crouch unblest at Superstition's feet.
Her hath he sent among ye; her, the pest
Of men below, and curse of Gods above:
Hers are the last worst tortures they inflict
On all who bend to any kings but them.
Born of Sicanus, in the vast abyss
Where never light descended, she survived
Her parent; he omnipotence defied,   200
But thunderstruck fell headlong from the clouds;
She tho' the radiant ether overpower'd
Her eyes, accustom'd to the gloom of night,
And quenched their lurid orbs, Religion's helm
Assuming, vibrated her Stygian torch,
Till thou, Astræa! tho' behind the Sire's
Broad egis, trembledst on thy golden throne.

THE PHOCÆANS

Preface

The Phocæans were a nation of Ionia, who founded several cities, in Italy, in Sicily, in Corsica, and in Gaul. Their war with a prince of the latter country, where they afterwards built Marseilles, is the main subject of this poem. The circumstances described in the following extracts are historically true. On leaving Phocæa, which Harpagus, the general of Cyrus, was besieging, and who, afraid of driving them to despair, is said to have connived at their departure, they threw into the sea a mass of burning iron, and swore that, until it should float, inextinguished, on the surface, they would never return. Their bravery in the cause of liberty, they thought, would entitle them to the protection of the Grecian states. But, what they in vain expected from their allies, was afforded them at the court of Arganthonius in Spain. In their voyage to Gaul they were attacked by Carthaginians, whom, tho' unequal in number of ships, they totally defeated. This gives the poem its first important movement; but as there is no allusion to it here, it is sufficient just to mention it. The whole of their history, that is extant, may be comprised in a very few lines. I shall be able to blend with it some actions of other nations, with which tho' they were relatively, they were not immediately concerned. These actions will promote the catastrophe, and heighten the interest, of the poem. But, I have not perfected my plan. It even is possible that the greater part of the *first* extract may be rejected. This, instead of a reason for witholding it, is a very sufficient one, with me, for it's insertion. The celebrated historian of the *Decline and Fall of the Roman Empire* has informed us how many times he recommenced that work, before he acquired the *key and tone* most proper for his performance; and we all recollect the story of a painter, no less celebrated, who exhibited one of his pictures for the express and sole purpose that the public might mark it's defects. For my part, I wish to ascertain not merely whether the poetry be good, but whether it be wanted—whether so much of the Iberian affairs be proper in this place, on any condition? For the *second* I make no apology. Unless as an extract from an unpublished poem, it requires from me less solicitude than any thing else that I have ever written. The remainder I shall not continue, till I can visit the country where the scene is laid: since, for works of this nature, not poetry alone, but chorography too is requisite.

The Phocæans

Heroes of old would I commemorate.
Those heroes, who obeyed the high decree
To leave Phocæa, and erect in Gaul
Empire, the fairest heaven had e'er design'd;
And, borne amidst them, I would dedicate
To thee O Liberty the golden spoils.
For, Liberty, 'tis thou whose voice awakes
Their sons, from slumber in the setting beams
Of sceptered Power, and banishest from Earth
Tho' tardier than hell's heaviest cloud she move,   10
And leave behind the wizard cup and sword —
Circæan soul-dissolving Monarchy.

Say, daughters of Mnemosyne and Jove,
Speak, hearts of harmony! what sacred cause
United, so long sever'd, in debate,
Pallas and Neptune? 'twas when every god
Flew shuddering from the royal feast accurst,
With Ceres, most offended, these ordain
Th' eternal terror of proud thrones to rise:
Such among eastern states Phocæa stood,   20
Such, amid Europe's oaken groves retired.

Now had Priené mourn'd her murder'd swains,
Who late ascending Mycalé, released
The pipe, and sitting on the way-side crag
Temper'd the tabor to their roundelays:
Of brittle ivy, from the living stone
Stript off with haste, before their partners came,
Chaplets to ward off envy they combined,
To ward off envy, not to ward off death,
Nor to survive themselves: now with amaze   30
Meander, rising slow from sedgey bed,
Sees soaring high the white-wing'd multitude
Of cranes and cycnets, like a sunny cloud,
Nor till they circle lower, distinguishes
The aerial blue between, and feeble cries
From thin protended throat: Pactolus tore
His yellow hair with human blood defiled,
And spurn'd his treacherous waves and tempting sand.

Of cities, built by heroes, built by Gods,
Throughout the Ægean, Asia now surveyed   40
None but Phocæa free: her bolder youth
The galling yoke of gifted peace disdain.
On far Iberia's friendly coast arrived,
Rich streamers, snatched from conquest, they display;
And Persic spoils, in sportive mockery worn,
Flutter and rustle round the steeds, that rear'd
Amid the caverns of the genial winds.

On Tagrus' top, start side-long from the tide.
All are advanced to manhood for the hour.
With sweet solicitude and fearful joy,   50
Each mother from the shaded ship descries
Her son amid the contest, and her son
Or now excels each rival in the race,
Or if behind them will ere long excel.
Naarchus, whose attemper'd hand heaven-taught,
Directed thro' wide seas and wearying straits
To rich Tartessus the Phocæan sails,
Now, leaning back against a stranded skiff,
Drawn till half upright on the shelving beach,
Turns idly round the rudder in it's rest,
And hardly thinks of land; warm youth attracts,   60
As amber sweet, the wither'd reed of age.
Such, on the banks of Hermus, on the banks
Of that most pleasant of all sacred streams,
For 'twas the nearest to his native home,
And first that exercised his crooked oar,
Now distant, swelling forth with sweet regrets! —
Such was Naarchus! steadfastly he gazed,
And harmless envy heav'd one mindful sigh.

Meanwhile, with Euxenus, and Hyelus,   70
In council sage, but stricken sore by years,
And Cimos, firm in friendship, firm in fight,
And more, whose wisdom, and whose bravery,

The hallowed bosom of but few records,
Men, high in nature, high in sphere, of souls
That burn in battle, or that shine in peace —
Protis, the son of Cyrnus, in the halls
Of Arganthonius, suppliant, thus implores
His peace, and his protection.

                        "Mighty king,
If ever thou injuriously hast borne   80
The rage of ruthless war, and surely war
Hath envied, and hath visited, a realm
So flourishing, so prosperous, behold
The scattered ruins of no humble race."
    Amid these words, a little from the ground
He rais'd his aching eyes, and waved his hand
Where over citron bowers and light arcades
Hung the fresh garlands fluttering from the mast:
Then paused; the hoary monarch, stung with grief,
Sate silent, and observ'd the frequent tear   90
Flow bitterly from off each manly cheek,
Uninterrupted! for the hero's soul
Flew back upon his country's wrongs, and grown
Impatient of the pity it required,
Sunk into sorrow: thus, his foes had said,
Had foes e'er seen him thus, the helpless child
Putting one arm against it's mother's breast,
Holds out the other to a stranger's hand,
But, ere receiv'd, it weeps: th' Iberian king

Then answer'd,
                    "Just and holy are the tears   100
Of warriors; sweet as cassia to the Gods,
To man and misery they're the dew of heaven.
But wherefor thus disconsolate! this arm
Might heretofore have rescued and avenged,
And now perhaps may succour." He embraced
The stranger, and, embracing him, perceived
His heart beat heavy thro' his panting vest;
Then thus continued, "we too have endured
Insulting power, insatiate avarice,
But ere the wrongs we suffer'd half were told   110
The sun, more rapid now his rays decline
Would leave the Atlantic wave."
                              The patriot chiefs,
Around, burn each to hear his own exploits
And see the history open on his name.
Fain would they seize congenial glances, fain
Force attestation from the question'd eye:
So pants for Glory, Virtue nurst by war,
That, some amongst them to their neighbours turn
Not for their neighbours notice but their king's.

    Hymneus was present, of Milesian race,   120
But he disdain'd his country, and preferr'd
One struggling hard with tyranny, to one
Where power o'er slaves was freedom and was rights,

Nor man degraded could but man degrade.
The harp, his sorrow's solace, he resumed,
Whose gently agitating liquid airs
Melted the wayward shadow of disgrace,
And, bearing highly up his well-stored heart
Above the vulgar, bade him cherish Pride. —
Mother of virtues to the virtuous man,   130
Her brilliant heavenly-temper'd ornaments
Tarnish to blackness at the touch of vice.
Sometimes the sadly quivering soul-struck wires
Threw a pale lustre on his native shore;
When suddenly the sound *"Conspirator"*,
How harsh from those we serve and those we love! —
Burst with insulting blow the enchanting strain,
And the fair vision vanish'd into air.
The pleasant solitude of sunny beach,
The yellow bank scoopt out with idle hands,   140
And near, white birds, and further, naked boys,
That, o'er the level of the lustrous sand,
Like kindred broods, seem ready to unite,
The tempest whirls away, — and where they stood
Up starts a monster, that, with hiss and howl,
Seizes the wretch who runs to loose it's chains.

    When Arganthonius saw him, he exclaim'd
"Hymneus! and thou too here! thy glowing words
  Could once, arousing in the warrior's breast

Enthusiastic rage, sublime the soul   150
So far above the rocks where Danger broods,
That she and all her monstrous progeny
Groveling, and breathing fire, and shadow-winged,
Become invisible.—O thou of power
With magic tones Affliction to disarm!
Thou canst conjure up fury, call down hope,
Or whisper comfort, or inspire revenge.
Rise! trace the wanderings of thy comrades, shew
What men, relying on the Gods, can bear."

He ended here, and Hymneus thus began.   160
"Long has Tartessus left her fertile fields,
And, but by forest beast or mountain bird,
Seen from afar her flocks lie unconsumed;
The maids of Sidon, and the maids of Tyre
To whom proud streams thro' marble arches bend,
Still bid the spindle urge it's whirring flight
And waft to wealth the luxury of our woes.
Thus without lassitude barbaric kings
Shall midst their revels read our history;
And thou too, warm to fancy, warm to grief.   170
In hall and arbour, shade and solitude,
Whose bosom rises at the faintest breath
From dizzy tower, dark dungeon, stormy rock,
But rises not, nor moves, to public pangs—
Woman! our well-wrought anguish shalt admire!

And toy-taught children overtake our flight.
But we have conquer'd:—hear me valiant youth!
Untired, and pressing for the course; O hear
Ye sires, whom stormy life's vicissitudes
At length, have driven on no hostile shore,   180
O hear me, nor repine; but cherish hope,
And fortune will return and cherish you.
We utter'd soothing words from sickening hearts,
And with firm voice in flight and rout proclaim'd
That we would never yield, would never fly:
While thus, revived by confidence, they rose,
Fortune gave weight to fancy's golden dreams,
And, more than hope dared promise, time perform'd.
Thus from some desert rock, which every tide
Drenches and deluges, the mariner   190
Marks the uneven surges rolling, marks
The black pods rattling as the wave retires,—
And now another!—high he folds his arms,
He groans, looks earnest on, and is resign'd.
Danger and safety this dread interval
Brings close; the billow self-suspended hangs;
The tide had reach'd it's highest, and has ebb'd:
While distant, now appearing, now unseen,
His comrades struggle up the fluited surge,
Their strength, their voices, wreckt! the spring approach'd;
The fields and woods were vocal with the joy
Of birds, that twittering from the thin-leav'd broom

Or close laurustin, or the sumach-tufts
Gay, nest-like, meditated nought but love.
Ah! happy far beyond man's happiness,
Who ever saw them wander o'er the waves
For guilty gold, or shiver on the shore
For life-wrung purple to array their breasts?
Theirs cherish, ours repudiate, chaste desire!
In vain was nature gay; in vain the flocks   210
With fond parental bleatings filled the fold;
In vain the brindled heifer lowed content
To crop the shining herbage, or to brouze
The tender maple in the twilight dell.
Cold, O ye flocks and herds, the hand will be
That fed ye, cold the hand that sweetly tuned
It's pipe to call ye to your nightly home,
Or gave the feebler dog encouragement
To drive the wolf away! vain care — the wretch
Who slew your shepherd, at the altar's horn   220
Slays you, to celebrate his victory.
    The Tyrians now approach; a thousand oars
Heave with impatient sweep the whitening surge
To seize Tartessus in the noon of peace.
The very zephyr now, that cool'd our coast,
Plays in the bosom of their sail, and smooths
Each rising billow; never more appall'd
The hind that cultivates Vesuvio's slope,
When with dull dash the firey tide o'erflows

The pumice that surrounds his humble cot,   230
Than was Tartessus. Olpis first espied
The naval host advancing; now delay
Were death;—he loosen'd the relapsing rope
From his left elbow, and the toils above
Dropt sounding on the surface of the waves.
He ran; nor enter'd he the city gate
Ere, interrupted oft, by haste, and fear,
In accents loud and shrill he thus began.
'Fly, fly, what madness holds you in your streets?
The Tyrians are behind; they climb the rocks   240
Light and unnumber'd as the brooding gulls.—
O fly, Tartessians! not a hope remains.'

     Incontinent, the noisy streets are fill'd
With young alike and old; the mother runs
To save her children, playing in the court,
Improvident of ill, and grasps their wrist,
Hurrying them onward, till they weep, and ask
'*For what?*' and whining plead the promised hour,
Now threaten loud, and now again in tears.
No more the murmuring labor of the loom   250
Detains the virgin, who, with patient hand,
But fluttering heart, the whitest vesture wove
For him she loved so tenderly, for him
Who soon arising from the nuptial couch,
Would scatter mid the warbling wanton choir

The lavish nuts, would hear their bland adieu,
And seize the pleasures they were taught to sing.
Here were the fathers sitting; they were seen
To wave their tremulous hand, and bid them go
Whose life is green and vigorous, 'for you   260
The sun will ripen many vintages,
But we are prone to tarry, cruel Tyre
Scarcely can drag the dying in her chains.'

        The throbs of urgent terror now subside
In all, and every one his earnest arms
With pious anguish throws around them, prays
To lead them into refuge, prays to strow
The bed of age, and close the beamless eye.
Alas! too confident in hoary hairs,
God's gift, but not God's blessing—they refuse   270
The proffer'd kindness; and their parted limbs
Hung upon hooks, with patriot gore distain'd
The wails they once defended! ah! thy day
Rolls on; a victim to the very sword
Thyself unsheathest, I behold thee fall;
Nor help is any near—that help; O Tyre!
Blind to the future, why hast thou destroyed?
Were it not better to extend the hand
T'ward rising states, than proudly crush them? realms
Which stand on ruins insecurely stand.   280
        But wherefor turn our eyes to other climes

Which fate has frown'd on! — tho' her frowns I dread,
I deem it first of human miseries
To be a tyrant, *then* to suffer one.
'Tis true, we left our city, left our fields,
O'er naked flints we travel'd, and review'd
What once we held so dear: the eye of youth
Saw, tho' the tear would often intervene,
And shake their branches, and suspend their bowers,
The groves that echoed to his horn, or waved   290
With gales that whilom whisper'd notes of love:
He saw; and linger'd long; for seldom fear
Invades a bosom harbouring regret.

      But others hasten'd to the far-off heights
Of Calpé: there a hundred grottoes gleam
High-archt with massy spar; and hence descend
Columns of crystal, ranged from side to side
In equal order; there the freshest Nymphs
Bring water sweet, and glide away unseen.
But hither few arrive, now darkness reigns   300
Around; but weary of the slow-paced hours
One lifts his eyes above, and, trembling, views
The moss and ivy shake with every wind
Against the yawning cavern; every wind
He deems a spectre's yell; and every beam
Shed from the clouded orbit stops his flight.
One, when molested from their lone abode
The birds of omen rise aloft in air,

Shrill-shrieking, and on whirring pinion borne
Sidelong, and circling o'er the pinnacles,   310
In turbid agitation thinks he hears
His infant, faintly wailing, or his wife
From far, imploring help he cannot give;
And wishes he were dead, yet fears to die.
'Twere piteous now, had pity past ourselves,
To hear sometimes the long-drawn moan of dogs,
Sometimes their quick impatience, while they sought
Fond master, left behind, or headlong dash'd
Where faithless moonshine fill'd the abrupt abyss.
From waken'd nest, and pinion silence-poiz'd,   320
Th' huge vulture drops rebounding;—first he fears;
Looks round; draws back; half lifts his cow'ring wing
Stretches his ruffled neck and rolling eye,
Tasts the warm blood, and flickers for the foe.

    Some, seated on the soft declivity,
Sink into weary slumber; others climb
The crumbling cliff, and craggy precipice,
To none accessible but him who fears.
Thus, to the mountain-brake, that overhangs
A valley dark and narrow, flies the kid   330
Before a lion: he from far espies
The pensile fugitive, nor dares pursue;
But gazing often, with tremendous roar
Shakes from his thirsty throat the fretful foam.

Here, love, ambition, labor, victory,
Injustice, vengeance, Hercules forgot,
Forgot how proud Laomedon, from Troy's
High summits, knew the hero, knew the steeds
That paw'd the plain beneath, and all the king
Shrunk, and the perjurer alone remain'd.   340
Here mournful Thessaly no more occur'd,
Deserted by her shepherds, while the neck
Of roving oxen soften'd from the yoke.
Here hospitable Scyros he forgot;
Here Tempé, fresh with springs, with woods embower'd;
Larissa too, whose glowing children vied
In pæans, vied in tracing where the throng
Around the quiver, markt the hand, of strength
To lift on high the shafts of Hercules.
While thro' the bulrushes the hero stept,   350
Slow, and intently looking round him, waved
His torch, and blue-eyed Lerna, lily-crownd,
Shook at the shadow of a future God.
'Twas there he started, matchless in the race;
The race was run; and Calpé was the goal.

      'Twas here Tartessus, in distraction fled
Before the steel of Sidon; she with Tyre
Unfurl'd the sail of conquest, Oceans rose
To waft her, suns to strow the yielding way.
Here were the realms of Night—each star was hers.   360
But Venus far above the rest, whose orb's

Meek lustre, melting thro' the cedar-sprays
That spire around the lofty Lebanon,
Led forth their matrons all at evening's close
To celebrate the sad solemnity.
There they abided: here, ill-omen'd hour!
Aside Lacippo's stream, with boughs o'erhung,
Dark alder, pearly-blossom'd arbutus,
And myrtle, highest held of earthly flowers,
And mixt with amaranth at the feasts above —   370
Maids snowy-stoled, and purple-mitred boys,
Foregoing each young pleasure — mazy dance,
Where Love most often but most slightly wounds,
Games, where Contention strives to look like Love
Scatter anemonies, and roses, torne
Ere daylight wakes them, from their mossy cell.

    Not thus, Nebrissa, went thy mountaneers.
Mad with religious lust and solemn wine,
They panted for their orgies, at the fount
Accustom'd: part the mangled heifer tear;   380
Part, stamping on the neck, wrench off it's brow
The horns, and blow them bubbling hoarse with blood
Some gird themselves with adders: others yell
From pipe far-screeching — trill above their head
The tymbrel — clash the cymbal — others drum
The hollow deeptoned Corybantine brass.
Before them, Sycus and Amphyllion,

Glad to have mixt themselves with men, at hours
When fearful childhood is constrain'd to rest,
Ran tripping for Lacippo; but to see   390
Flowers, that profusely floated down the stream,
Breaking the yellow moonshine as they passed,
Surprized and held them; fixt on this, they heard
No plaintive strain beyond: for childhood's mind
Sits on the eyeball; 'tis her boundary.
But, higher up, those who the orgies led
Hearken'd, at every pause, and each was fill'd
With clear responses winding thro' the vale.

      Old Cheratægon chided this delay.
'Why stood they gaping? had the wrathful Moon   400
Struck them? had any Satyr from the heights,
Had he whom every Season stops to crown,
Whom Hellespontic Lampsacus adores,
Answer'd their carols, kind? if so — reply.'
Then, placing to his lips the clarion,
He started, waved it round, and listening
Again, cried out '*a female voice I hear,
Proceed, proceed.*' They hurry on; they view
The choir: the shrieking damsels cannot fly;
Their vesture baffles each attempt of fear.   410
In vain implore they Venus, and adjure
By all she suffer'd when Adonis died,
The rustics knew Adonis not by name

Nor Venus by a tear. They wring their hands
In agony, they clasp them in despair,
Or, those restricted in the strong embrace,
Raise praying eyes to heaven, and bend the neck
Back till, it's tapering column quite convulsed,
The breasts that from their marble sanctuary
Stood out, inviting Chastity and Love,   420
By violence and passion are profaned.

     While tumult rages there and wild affright,
Led by avenging deities, and warm'd
With patriot fire, the purest that ascends
Before the presence of those deities,
The caverns we had left, and many a plain
As desolate, where now the wolf, enraged,
Bit the deserted fences of the fold;
And now with plighted faith and pledging vows
Throughout invoke our murder'd countrymen: 430
For now at last the radiant host of heaven
Seem'd, going one by one, to delegate
Peace and repose behind; these oft enchant
The wicked; but whene'er the weary lids
Drop, either dreadful visions they inclose,
Tenacious, or the senseless breast imbibes
The poison'd balm of sweet security.
Seen thro' that porch's pillars, yonder wood
Tho' not far distant, yet from hence appears

More like a grassy slope — by Lybian blasts   440
Distorted — there in ambush, we surveyed
Our battlements, whose friendly shadow stretch'd
O'er half the ruins of old Geryon's tomb:
When silently and quick athwart the dale
Glide ranks of helmets; these alone are seen,
Darkness and distance occupy the rest.
They fade away, and eagerly we catch
The rumour of their march: the hunter, worn
With service, dragging some ignoble weight,
Stops in the passing wind the well-known cry   450
Of hound that, after hard-run chase, hath lept
Up to his nostrils, or against his side
Rested one foot — the other gall'd with thorns —
Like him we, conscious of our former strength,
Quake with the impotence of wild desire.

   Less dangerous now is our determined course
Toward Tartessus: we approach the walls;
We reach them; nor had halted, ere the gates
Fly open: starting at the prodigy,
Encouraged at the fact, the Iberian bands   460
Rush in, and with a dreadful shout proclaim
The vengeance of the Gods; afraid to strike
At first, lest any one of these, conceal'd
In human likeness, at the portal placed,
The force, himself inspired them with, bewail.
Astounded and aghast, the Tyrians rise

From slumber: these imagine it a dream,
Discrediting their senses' evidence;
Those in the portico cry out to arms,
Forgetful of their own, while many, driven   470
By desperation, reckless of their shield
Or buckler, rush amidst us, sword in hand,
Impetuous, covering with their prostrate corse
The spot they fought on: others, overthrown
By numbers pressing forward, under throngs
Of enemies, groan loud; a double pang
Such feel, in dying with no hostile wound.
Hundreds, and fortunate are they, prolong
Sleep into death, nor ever know the change.
The remnant in their hollow ships confide
For refuge, close pursued; thrice happy few   480
Who now, the pitchy, hard, and slippery side
Surmounted, mindless yet of sail or oar,
Embrace their own Patæcus[1] on the prow.
O'er their companions, in the crouded strand

1. The Patæci were little images, like those which the Spaniards, and
others of the same religion, carry about with them at present, to avert
calamity. I imagine that those charms and amulets which are also in
use among the nations of Africa, and which are called *fetiches*, are of
the same origin: they perhaps are the prototypes of the Patæci, and were
introduced into Spain by the Carthaginians. When the Tyrians are mentioned here, they must be supposed in great part, Carthaginians; as the
people of the United States of America were, during their alliance, indis-
criminately called Englishmen, by our enemies.

Death, leading up night's rear, her banner waves,
Invisible, but rustling like the blast
That strips the fallen year: with arms outstretched,
Dismay, before her, pushes on; and Fear
Crouching unconscious close beside her, casts   490
A murky paleness o'er her wing black-plumed.
Just liberated from their noisom cells,
Slavery's devoted, thirsting for revenge,
Drink deep; the fetter is at last become
An instrument of slaughter, and the feet
Swoln with it, bathe themselves in hostile blood,
Till from the vallies deep the fogs arise
Perceptible; while, on the summits, Mora
Her saffron robe and golden sceptre lays.
Then of their lofty vessels we descry   500
Nought save the topmost sails, each nether part
By Gades, tho' behind them, was obscured;
These, distant yet, seem'd o'er the town displayed.

     'Tis painful, O Phocæans, to unfold
The brazen gates of war, and find Revenge
Bursting her brittle manacles, while Rage
Strikes with impatient spear the sounding floor.
Here Scycus and Amphyllion I behold,
Shivering, and with the back of feeble wrist
Drawn frequently across their swolen eyes,   510
Wiping large tears away—poor harmless pair!

You, playing near life's threshold, strown with flowers,
Common indeed, but sweet, and all your own,
Death snatcht away, and flapt her raven wing.

    The Tyrians sally forth, to meet the hour
When woe and darkness yield to light and glee,
And reach Lacippo's fount ere earliest dawn.
No mortal meet they, nor the faintest noise
Hear, but of rustling leaves and tinkling rill.
They wonder; look around them; shudder, seize   520
Each zephyr, and each shadow, which he makes
By nimbly lighting on the pliant boughs
Creep further on the grass: for every man
Imagines, tho' all other may have strayed,
Surely his own must near him still remain.
But all upon the distant hills were drag'd
Thro' wild and winding sheepwalks, into huts
Where, with unsated eye, Nebrissan wives,
Not yet suspicious of supplanting charms,
Survey their strange attire: one draws the veil   530
Aside, and fancies somewhat in the face
Tho' foreign, like her countrywomen; lips
Rosy, but rather blighted; eyes full-orbed
Ringlets that o'er pellucid temples wave,
As cedars o'er steep snow-drifts; blooming cheeks;
But, courted not by sun or sea-born gale,
Pallid and puny when compared with hers:

Another, hath some broken flower escaped
Mid the dishevel'd hair, with curious hand
Twists round, on tiptoe, it's exotic stem,   540
Exulting high with ingenuity.

      The Tyrians, now, disconsolate, unite
In counsel: each one differs in the way
To follow, each his neighbour's choice amends.
When on the pathway haply one espied
A torch; he whirl'd, he kindled it; he swore
By earth and heaven 'twas happy; he exclaim'd
'We too will sacrifice! Revenge be ours!
Revenge is worthy to succeed to Love.
Each irresistable, immortal each,   550
Not blind—the wretch feigns that—their pupils roll
In fire unquenchable: Pursuasion form'd
Their lips, and raptured at their lively hue
She kist her new creation; hence delight
Breathes thro' the thirsting fibres of the breast,
Like honey from Dodona's prophet-grove,
Sweet and inspiring too—Revenge, revenge.'
Silence dwelt shortly with them, ere he touched
This jarring nerve; when suddenly their hearts
Vibrated into dreadful unison.   560
They gape upon him, gathering from his breath
(As manna from the desert men would seize,)
The substance of their wishes; they demand

In sentences imperfect, how to grasp
The phantom set before them, whispering
With eager but with hesitating haste
Together, and awaiting no reply:
Nay, often an enquiry, that commenced
With one, concluded in another's ear.
They moved; the croud seem'd growing: swift they strode
Toward the streamlet, thither where it sprad,
Wider, and (as upon it's bosom fell
The frigid, iron-color'd, unripe light)
Just trembled: here the boy Amphyllion
Stood waiting for the broken garlands, borne
No farther by the current; forward lean'd
The busy idler, under where he stood
Sweeping them gently on with willow wand.
He thought, full sure he thought—such eagerness
His one protended and one poising hand,   580
Half-open lips, and steady lustrous eyes,
Show'd plainly—safe arrived ere others woke,
To deck his mother's door, and be forgiven.
Sycus more weary, on his arm inclined,
Sat peevish by, and, often of the way
Complaining, yet unwilling to arise,
Bit acid sorrels from their juicy stalk.
'Lo yonder!' he exclaim'd, 'the morning dawns
Among the junipers, and ill forebodes
Beside such dampness when no dew has fallen—   590

This bursting glare, while all around is shade.
Can it be morning? no; *there* mornings rise:
It is not morning; and the moon is gone;
It cannot be the moon,' too rightly judged
Poor Sycus; nearer now flashed redder light
Than rising moons give reapers going home;
Now nearer, and now nearer yet, approach'd
Voices, and armour glimmer'd thro' the glade;
Next, helmets were distinguisht; lastly, vests
Black afar off, their proper crimson shew'd.   600
They tremble at the sight, and deadly drops
Trickle down ankles white like ivory.
Pity and mercy they implore — the soul
Presages ere it reasons — they implore
Pity and mercy, ere the enemy's hand
Seizes them, ere, in painful bondage bent,
Behind them hang so helplessly their own.

Uprooted smells the hazel underwood,
The verdant pile ascends; upon the top
Branches of pitch-tree are arranged, across,   610
And cover'd with their leaves: the cymbals ring;
The tymbrels rough, and doubling drums, reply.

Music, when thunders arm her heavenly voice,
May rouse most other passions — she may rouse
The Furies from their deep Tartarean dens,

Or Wonder from her unseen orbit, fixt
The middlemost of endless myriads—
Terror she stops amid his wild career,
Engages, and subdues. Amphyllion's heart
Flutter'd indeed but flutter'd less confined,   620
He trembled more, yet dreaded less: the boy
Would now with rapturous violence have rubbed
His palms to sparkling, were they but unbound,
His head he would have nestled in the lap
Of Fortune, when he found the budded spoils
Lie innocent, squared well, and garland-hung.
He laugh'd at their device; he look'd around,
And saw the knife, but sought the sacrifice.

    Can you, etherial Powers! if any rule
Above us or below, or if concern   630
For human sins and sorrows touches you—
Can you see, quivering, shrinking, shrivelling,
Lips without guile, and bosoms without gall,
Nor pity, succour, save! alas, your will
Was pleaded, and your presence was invoked.
First, 'twas revenge—but, when 'twas done, 'twas heaven!
When others rise in anger, men exclaim
'Fierce Furies urge them:' but when they themselves,
'Righteous inflexible Eumenides.'
Even thou, Venus! Goddess! even thou,   640
That leadest the Gætulian lioness

From caves and carnage, and on sunny sands
Makest to slumber with satiety—
Thou wreathest serpents as thou wreathest flowers,
Thou silencest the winds without a word,
Thou curbest the black Tempest; and the face
Of Ocean brightens at thy filial smile,
Yet, either thou art cruel or profaned.

When Cruelty and Youth together dwell
Nature may weep indeed! they also wept.   650
The sons of Tyre and Sidon also wept.
Returning to the gates, they only heard
A few last groans, only a few fond names
Given them long ago: by madness driven,
Like Atys, when he left his father's home,
Never to see it more, nor to admire
His face dim-shining from his olived thigh—
They run into the woods, and are devour'd
By grief and famine, without friend or grave.

The cormorants have flown across the strait,   660
Some wealth they carried off, the best remains.
Confidence in ourselves, in them distrust.
By the wise serpent, wisdom we are taught.
We see the hugest of the reptile race
Uncoil to crush, beslaver to devour,
No longer we relie on Punio faith.

But walls and watchtowers raise along the coast
And fortify stout ships with hearts as stout."   668

        Here ended Hymneus: and the hall awhile   1
Was silent, Arganthonius then arose.
"My honored guests! who bravely have endured
The toils of exil and the storms of war,
It will add little to your weariness,"
Said he, "if ye will trace to us the ways
By land and sea ye have gone thro, before
Ye reacht the port wherein ye now shall rest."

Then Protis, he who led them, thus replied:
"O King! the stranger finds in thee a friend   10
Who found none in his kindred. But reproach
Better becomes the weak than firmer breast.
We will not turn to those who past us by
In the dark hour: from such and from the land
Where Pelops, in the days of heroes, reigned,
        We turn to Delphi; we consult the God;   1
The God, omniscient Phœbus, thus replies.
'Long have your wanderings been o'er wearying seas,
And long o'er earth, Phocæans, must they be —
Where war shall rage around you, treachery lurk,
And kings and princes struggle hard from peace.'
I never shall forget that awful hour,
When Consolation fled Calamity,

And Hope was slow to leave the Delphic shrine.
Scarce half the steps surmounted, sprang the roof;   10
The gorgeous walls grew loftier every step;
In gracile ranks of regular advance
The melting pillars rose like polisht air:
The floor too, seem'd ascending, seemed to wave
It's liquid surface like the heaven-hued sea;
Throughout reflecting, variously displayed,
Deviceful piety and massive prayers.
Above the rest, beside the altar, stood
The Sardian vases, gift of Crœsus, one
Of beaten silver, one of burnished gold,   20
Dazzling without, but dark from depth within.
Alas! for these Ecbatana[2] should have bowed
Her seven-fold shield, and Lydian flames dissolved
The yielding iris of the embattled crown.
Too soon hath Crœsus found, that once impell'd
By headlong folly or obdurate fate,
All Delphi's tripods, censers, gems, high-piled,
Cannot stop Fortune's swift-descending wheel.
Who but the maniac, then, would strain his throat
And rack his heart beneath capricious birds,   30

2. The walls of Ecbatana were built by Deioces. They were seven in
number, and each of a circular form. Each was also raised gradually
above the other, just as much as the battlements were high, and all
were of different colors. The first, which equalled in circumference the
city of Athens, was white, from the base of the battlements: the second,
black: third, purple: fourth, blue: fifth, orange: sixth, silver: seventh, gold.

And tear disaster from it's bowel'd bed!
I hung o'er these proud gifts, and, rising, felt
A cold hoarse murmur chide the inconscious sigh.
The people heard with horror the decree,
They were undone — and, who himself undo?
This comes from wisdom; woe betide the wise!
Why should they thus consult the oracle
When it could give them only toil and grief?
These were inclined to penance, those to rage.
O how near Nature Folly sometimes leads!   40
Penance seem'd bending with sororial care
To raise the brow of pale Despondency;
And Rage arous'd them, gave them energy,
Made them unjust, perhaps, but made them great.
Not in one city, could we long remain
Ere there occur'd some signal which approved
The Delphic revelation: was the crow
Heard on the left, was thunder on the right,
The starts of terror met the scoffs of scorn.
Taunt, accusation, contumely, curse,   50
Questioning stamp and pale-lipt pious sneer,
Confusion, consternation, mystery,
Procession, retrogression, vortexes
Of hurry, wildernesses of delay:
Each element, each animal, each glance,
Each motion, now, admonish'd them, each bird
Now bore the thunder of almighty Jove,

Each fibre trembled with Phocæa's fate.
Our parting sails far other prospects cheer'd.
Self-courteous Pride, awaiting courtesy,   60
Charm'd with bland whispers half our pangs away.
What Grecian port that would not hail our ships?
'Twas oft debated which high-favor'd land
Should share the honors it might well confer.
Some from Cecropian Athens traced our line,
And said "Minerva's city shall rejoice."
Some Sparta lures—perfection fancy-form'd!
So pure her virtue, and her power so poised,
With Asia's despot how could Sparta join?
Now, from Eurotas driven, whose willows wove   70
His knotty cradle, where should Freedom fly!
Could Freedom exiled cherish exiled Hope?
We leave the plains, then, where the sports and flowers
Are faint, untinged with blood; where naked feet
The mountain snow and woodland hoar condense,
And virgin vestures crack the margent grass.
Resolv'd no longer faithless friends to seek,
And not renouncing, yet, the oracle;
Not yet forgetting, that, from Greece expell'd,
War was to rage around us—could there aught   80
Be markt so plainly as the Enusian isle:
So near our native land too! all exclaim
There take we refuge: here we take revenge.
Again we trust the winds and tempt the waves;

Again behold our country—first ascends
Melæna's promontory, frowning dark,
And threatening woe to foreign mariners.
Now lengthen out thy light unwarlike walls,
And, as the clouds fly over thee or lower,
Leucas! so glance they forward or retire.   90
Myrina next, and Cumæ, and, beyond,
Larissa—nearer still, yet stands unseen,[3]
(If ought be standing of her blest abodes)
Phocæa: yes!—air, sea, and sky, resound
'Phocæa!'—honor'd o'er the Gods was he
Who the first temple's faintest white descried.
What tears of transport, shouts of extasy,
O what embraces now! foul Enmity
At that sweet sound flew murmuring far away,
And the proud heart the precious moment seized   100
To burst the brutal chains itself imposed.
Dear native land! last parent, last—but lost!
What rivers flow, what mountains rise, like thine?
Bold rise thy mountains, rich thy rivers flow,
Fresh breathes thy air, and breathes not o'er the free!
Love, vengeance, sweet desires, and dear regrets,
Crowded each bosom from that pleasant shore:
We touch the extremest shadow of it's hills,

3. Phocæa stands at the furthest end, and at a *curviture*, of the bay,
on the borders and *front* of which are Cumæ, Myrina, and Larissa—
the first objects that appear.

And taste the fragrance of their flowering thyme.
We see the enemy; we hear his voice;   110
His arrows now fly round us; now his darts:
We rush into the port with pouncing prow.
Faint ring the shields against our hooked poles;
We dash from every pinnace, and present
A ridge of arms above a ridge of waves.
Now push we forward; now, the fight, like fire,
Closes and gapes and gathers and extends.
Swords clash, shields clang; spears whirr athwart the sky,
And distant helmets drop like falling stars.
Along the sands, and midst the rocks, arise   120
Cries of dismay and cries of plangent pain;
Shouts of discovery, shouts of victory—
While, seen amid the ranks, and faintly heard,
Thunders the bursting billow's high-archt bound.
They flee; we follow: where the fray retreats
Torrents of blood run down, and mark it's course,
And seize the white foam from the scatter'd sand,
And bear it floating to the sea unmixt:
While many a breathless corse of warrior bold
Dashes, with hollow sullen plunge, beneath   130
The hostile gods dark-frowning from our prows.

   O how delightful to retrace the steps
Of childhood! every street, and every porch
And every court, still open, every flower

Grown wild within! O worse than sacrilege
To tear away the least and lowliest weed
That rears it's wakeful head between the stones!
He who receiv'd undaunted, and surveyed
With calmly curious eye the burning wound,
And open'd and inspected it, shed tears   140
Upon the deep-worn step, before the gate,
That often whetted, once, his trusty sword.

    The trumpet calling, the Phocæan barks
Reach, with reluctant haste, the Enusian shore.
Here the good Prodicus, whose prudent eye
Foresaw that we were giving to the winds
Our inconsiderate sail, and who advised
To seek our safety from the Delphic shrine,
Died! — those who living fill'd the smallest space
In death have often left the greatest void.   150
The honest crew was gloomy; thro' such gloom
We best discern, and weigh, and value, tears.
When from his dazzling sphere the mighty falls,
Men, proud of shewing interest in his fate,
Run to each other and with oaths protest
How wretched and how desolate they are.
The good departs, and silent are the good.
Here none with labor'd anguish howl'd the dirge,
None from irriguous Ida, cypress-crown'd,
Blew mournfully the Mariandyne pipe;   160

Yet were there myrtles, polisht from the fleece
Of many flocks, successive, and the boughs
Of simple myrtle twined his artless bier.
Some scoopt the rock, some gather'd wonderous shells;
Warm was their study, warm were their disputes;
This was unpolisht; this unsound; 'twas askt
With finger bent, and drawing tacit shame,
Were shells like that for men like Prodicus?
Respect drew back, dishearten'd; Reverence paused:
To features harsh and dark clung first-born tears,   170
And fond contention soften'd where they fell.
Amid these funerals, four aged men
Came out of Chios; olive in their hands,
Around their shoulders flow'd the Persic robe.
They said, report had reacht the Chian state
Of our arrival at it's subject isles;
That, before Cyrus, at his footstool, sworn
In war his soldiers as his slaves in peace,
Charged with the king's high mandate they appear'd.
He said—'Obey me, and ye still retain   180
Freedom; ye loose it when ye disobey.
Therefor ye Grecian states of Asia's realm,
Should ye presume to countenance my curse,
Or dare to sucour him whom I disclaim,
Mark me aright, ye perish! go, demand,
Ye men of Chios, if the isle be yours,
That those who late escaped our scymetar,

Fly thence, or bend submissive to our sway.
Should they resist, or hesitate, the fleet
Of every city, from the Sestian stream   190
To Gaza, shall attack them, or pursue,
Nor furl the sail till conquest crown the mast.'

    To whom Pythermus, bursting from the throng.
'Go, tell thy master, go, thou self-bound slave,
Thou subject![4] soon his dreaded foe departs.
Give him this opiate that thy hoary hairs
Have gather'd from the way—but neither fear
Of Persian swords nor Chian ships will urge
Fresh flight, but famine dire from friends dismayed.
We want not protestations: spare to lift   200
Those eyes to heaven that roll in vows disolved,
Those ready hands that trembling creak with wreaths;
Were not those hands against right counsel rais'd
Were they not joined before the conqueror's throne?
Phocæans venerate not empty age;

---

4. It will probably be thought that, after calling any one a *self-bound slave*
the word *subject* could hardly be used as a term of severe reproach. But it
must also be recollected what people these Phocæans were: that in their
hostility to *regular governments*, particularly to that of Cyrus, who gener-
ously offered to take them under his *protection*, they were so fierce and
refractory as in the paroxism of their rage and folly to have reasoned
thus—Subjects are by convention what slaves are by compulsion: slaves
are unwilling subjects, subjects are willing slaves—they must indeed
have reasoned thus, before they could have used any such expression.

Age for the ark of virtue was designed,
And virtuous how they value, best declare
These rites, these robes, and, look around, these tears.
Hast thou forgotten how when Thales spake,
Best of the good and wisest of the wise,   210
And bade aloud the colonies unite
In Teios, middlemost of Asia's marts,
Against his equable and sound demand
Ye stood, and bargain'd freedom for a bale.
Else federal faction and rich rivalry
Had murmur'd, but flow'd down; equality
Had lessen'd danger and diffused success;
And inland Temperance and mountain Strength
Cherisht those arts which Avarice confined—
Confined for riot, ravishment, and spoil.   220
The fruit of commerce, in whatever clime,
Ripening so sweet, so bitter in decay,
Enervates, pampers, poisons, who partake:
Thine, Freedom! rais'd by Toil and Temperance,
Bright as the produce of the Hesperian isles,
Fills the fond soul with sweet serenity,
And mortals grow immortal from it's shade.

     O from what height descend I to ourselves!
Alas, for Chios swore our fates to share.
Heaven grant oblivion to the ungenerous race   230
Who spum'd that Liberty their fathers clasp'd

With extacy, with madness, with despair—
For sure they thought such blessing was not man's
They felt 'twas theirs—and love was jealousy.
O people, lost to glory, lost to shame,
Neglect the living, but respect the dead,
Your fathers' ghosts the breaking bond will hear.
But, heavenly Powers! whose silent orbs controul
The balanced billows of the boundless sea,
Who framing all things, o'er each state preside,   240
And, ruling all things, rule man's restless heart.—
O! if your servant, still, for follies past,
Unconscious faults, or vices unatoned,
Must suffer,—wander still, still groan repulse,
Ne'er, Powers of Mercy! may from kindred hand
But from the fiercest foe that arrow fly
The men of Chios heard him, and retired.
Again come groundless fears and dark debates.
Part is undaunted; swearing to abide
The threats of Cyrus, anchor'd in the bay: 250
Others walk near, and o'er the crowd descry
The hoary heights of storied Sipylus;
And every tufted lair and tripping stream
Comes from afar before the fondling eye,
Well they remember how the moulten mass
Of ardent iron from Hephestus' fane
Was plung'd into the port, and how they swore
They and their children, while the struggling fire

Seiz'd the white column of the crumbling wave,
That sooner should it rise again, and glow   260
Upon the surface, than would they return,
Or e'er, tiara'd Median, bend to thee.
Now it repents them, now it grieves them! years
Are more, and hopes are fewer! they withdraw
One after one, slow creeping to the coast,
Firm against oaths, and fixt to be forsworn.
This when the braver, better part beheld,
First with entreaties, then with threats, they try
To turn the coward counsel back in time:
Those, so intent on ruin, so resolved   270
Against compulsion and against consent,
Would fight their brethren while they court their foe.
Stung by disdain and anguish, I exclaim'd
'What would ye more encounter? ye have borne
War, exile, persecution; would ye bear
(O last calamity of minisht man!)
The hand of pardon on your abject head?
Disease, affliction, poverty, defeat,
Leaving behind them unadopted shame,
Stamp not thus basely low the breathing clay.   280
Man bend to man!—forbid it righteous heaven!
T' endure each other hard calamity
Is great, is glorious; others are from high.
Let us contend in these who best can bear,
Contend in that who bravest can withstand.'

Again, appearing shadowingly, return
Spirit, and mild remorse, and decent pride:
The young that waver'd, turn their eyes, and find
Most still unmoved—enough that most remain.
Slow, and abasht, and silent, they rejoin   290
Their bold companions; timorous age believes
They just return to bid their friends farewel:
They join; and unsuspicious youth believes
They only went to bid the old adieu.
None are so stedfast in the servile strife,
As those who, coldly pious, closely draw
The cowl o'er failings from themselves conceal'd;
Who deeming oaths most sacred, deem that oaths
Are made and broken by the same decree:
Wroth at each light-paced laughing folly's name,   300
They lay a nation's counsel'd crimes on heaven:
They think they worship, while they wrong, the Gods,
And think they pity, while they hate, mankind.
With these go all who, reckoning in themselves
Unfavor'd wealth or wisdom undiscern'd,
Are grown disdainful to have met disdain;
Who, spurning most from others what they most
Hug in themselves, and feed to plethory,
Join stubborn patience with intolerant zeal.
These were the men, who, when the tyrant came   310
Against their country and their freedom, call'd
Debate sedition, acquiescence peace.

Twelve barks, for twelve sufficed them, were decreed
To bear away infirmity and fear,
And falsehood from the crew—twelve feeble barks—
Twice thirty more of stoutest bulk remain.
With these we, buoyant on unbounded hopes,
Ocean's vast wilds by friendly stars retrace.
First, vows and offerings to the powers above,
And to Poseidon, last, were duly paid: 320
Nor seldom, when we saw the cynosure,[5]
Thales! the grateful heart thy name recall'd.
Blest above men, who gainedst from the Gods
Power, more than heroes, tho' their progeny,
Power over earth, power over sea and sky.
They gave thee wisdom—this thou gavest men,
They gave thee Virtue—this too thou wouldst give:
They called thee aside, and led thy steps
Where never mortal steps were led before,
And shew'd the ever-peaceful realm of light.   330

5. According to Diogenes Laertius, the poet Callimachus had somewhere
attributed to Thales the first discovery, or rather, I should suppose, the
first application to any nautical purpose, of the ursa Minor. Whether the
mariners observed the Cynosure or Helicé—

> "Ex his altera apud Graios *Cynosura* vocatur,
>   Altera dicitur esse Helice"—

their remembrance of Thales would be natural. I have preferred the cynosure as the most obvious. The quarter from which they sailed must also
be considered. *Major* Pelagis apta, Sidoniis *minor*. (Seneca)—

>   Regit altera Graias,
>   Altera Sidonias, utraque sicca, rates.

Amidst the Gods thou lookedst down on Earth —
(Their glory could absorb but half thy soul)
Thou lookedst down, and viewing from afar
Earth struggling with Ambition, didst implore
Now that another country must be sought,
And other counsel taken, (thine disdain'd)
That they would chain up danger from the night,
And strengthen with new stars the watery way.

With surer sail, the daring mariners,
Leaving the green Ægæan, isle-begem'd,   340
Explore the middle main: remembering Greece,
They swell with fiercer pride and fresh disdain;
They scorn the shelter of her mountain-tops,
They curse with closer teeth the bitter blast,
Nor hail the fairest gales that blow from Greece.

SEQUEL

O'erpast was warfare: youths and maidens came
From the Ligurian shore, and the Tyrrhene,
And the far Latian, to console the brave
After their toils, and celebrate the rites
Of the same Gods. Hymen stood up aloft;
His torch was brighter than the deadly glare
Lately so reverenced by a crouching throng
In Druid worship, over blacken'd oak
Leafless and branchless: hymns were sung before
That smiling youth whose marble brow was crown'd   10
With summer flowers, and Love's with earlier spring's.
Apollo stood above them both, august,
Nor bent his bow in anger more than Love.
Here was no Python; worse than Python one
Had vext the land before his light came down.
Here stood three maidens, who seem'd ministers
To nine more stately, standing somewhat higher
Than these demure ones of the downcast smile:
Silent they seem'd; not silent all the nine.
One sang aloud, one was absorb'd in grief   20
Apparently for youths who lately bled;
Others there were who, standing more elate,
Their eyes upturn'd, their nostrils wide expanded,
Their lips archt largely; and to raise the hymn

Were lifted lyres; so seemed it; but the skill
Of art Hellenic forged the grand deceit.
Night closed around them, and the stars went down
Advising their departure: when they went
I too had gone, for without them I felt
I should be sad, when from above there came   30
A voice... it must have been a voice of theirs
It was so musical... and said, "Arise
Loiterer, and sing what thou alone hast heard."
"Inspire me then, said I, O thou who standest
With the twelve maidens round!"

                               Was it a dream?
I thought the Delian left his pedestal.
A living God, I thought he toucht my brow;
Then issued forth this hymn, the very hymn
I caught from the full choir, the last they sang,
"Incline a willing ear, O thou supreme   40
Above all Gods! Jove Liberator! Jove
Avenger! to Phocæa's sons impart
The gift of freedom all our days, and peace
To hold it sacred and with blood unstain'd.
And do thou, consort of the Omnipotent!
Bestow thy blessing on our rescued few,
And grant the race, adoring thee, increase."

POSTSCRIPT
TO *GEBIR*

Gebir in different quarters has been differently received. I allude not to those loyal critics, who, recently
mounted on their city-war-horse, having borrowed the
portly boots and refurbished the full-bottomed perukes of
the ancient French chevaliers, are foremost to oppose the
return of that traitor, whom, while he was amongst them,
Englishmen called Freedom, but now they have expelled
him, Anarchy: since, the very first *Reviews* of this Associ-
ation were instituted, not merely for parade but for hostility: not for exercise, correctness, and precision, so adventurous and impetuous were these conscripts, but for actual
and immediate battle. The *Critical* and *Monthly*, as being
of the old establishment, are those on which at present I
would fix attention. In respect to *Gebir*, the one perhaps is
conducted by a partial, but certainly by a masterly, hand.
It objects, and indeed with reason, to a temporary and
local obscurity, which I have not been able, or I have not
been bold enough, to remove: but never on the whole,
since it's first institution, has a poem been more warmly
praised. The other's account is short: containing one
quotation and two mis-statements. "That the poem was

nothing more than the version of an Arabic tale; and that the author, not content with borrowing the expressions, had made the most awkward attempts to imitate the phraseology of Milton." The Review is not before me. I believe I have softened, but I have not perverted, nor have I deteriorated his style. No man would make or meditate so rash indefencible an attack, unless he were certain that, if not already stationed there, he could speedily drop into obscurity. I repeat to him in answer, what I before asserted in my preface, that, so far from a *translation*, there is not a single sentence, nor a single sentiment, in common with the tale. Some characters are drawn more at large, some are brought out more prominent, and several are added. I have not changed the scene, which would have distorted the piece, but every line of appropriate description, and every shade of peculiar manners, is originally and entirely my own. Now, whether this gentleman has or has not read the poem, whether he has or has not read the romance, his account is equally false and equally malicious. For the romance is in english, therefor he could have read it; the poem is in english, and therefor he could have compared it. There is no disgrace in omitting to read them: the disgrace is, either in pretending to have done what he had not done, or in assuming a part which he was incompetent to support. But there *is* a disgrace in omitting to read Milton; there is a disgrace in forgetting him. The critic has not perused or not remembered him: it would be impossible, if he had, that he should accuse me of borrowing his expressions. I challenge him to produce them. If indeed I *had* borrowed them, so little should I have realized by the dangerous and wild speculation, that I might have composed a better poem and not have been a better poet. But I feared to break open, for the supply of my games or for the maintenance of my veteran heroes, the sacred treasury of the great republican. Although I might enjoy, not indeed the extorted, but the unguarded praise of an enemy, if my vanity could stoop so low and could live on so little,—of an enemy who, throughout so long a journey, and after so many speeches, and those on such various occasions, pertinaciously took me for Milton—I will add, for the information of my young opponent, what a more careful man would conceal, but what in his present distress will relieve him greatly, that this, which amongst the vulgar and thoughtless might currently pass for praise, is really none at all. For, the language of *Paradise Lost* ought not to be the language of *Gebir*. There should be the softened air of remote antiquity, not the severe air of unapproachable sanctity. I devoutly offer up my incence at the shrine of Milton. Woe betide the intruder that would steal it's jewels! It requires no miracle to detect the sacrilege. The crime will be found it's punishment. The venerable saints, and still more holy personages, of Raphael or Michael-Angelo, might as consistently be placed among the Bacchanals and Satyrs, bestriding the goats and bearing the vases of Poussin, as the resemblance of that poem, or any of it's component parts, could be introduced in mine. I have avoided high-sounding words. I have attempted to throw back the gross materials, and to bring the figures forward. I knew beforehand the blame that I should incur. I knew that people would cry out "your burden was so light, we could hardly hear you breathe, pray where is your merit." For, there are few who seem thoroughly acquainted with this plain and simple truth, that it is easier to elevate the empty than to support the full. I also knew the *body* of my wine, and that years must pass over it, before it would reach it's relish. Some will think me intoxicated, and most will misconstrue my good-nature, if I invite the Reviewer, or any other friend that he will introduce, — but himself the most earnestly, as I suspect from his manner that he *poetizes*—to an amicable trial of skill. —I will subject myself to any penalty, either of writing or of ceasing to write, if the author, who criticizes with the flightiness of a poet, will assume that character at once, and, taking in series my twenty worst verses, write better an equal number, in the period of twenty years. I shall be rejoiced if he will open to me any poem of my contemporaries, of my English contemporaries I mean, and point out three pages more spirited, I will venture to add more classical than the three least happy and least accurate in *Gebir*.

In challenging a comparison the discriminating will remark, that more expertness is used than bravery. They will certainly acquit me of presumption, altogether, and judge from the character of the person thus addressed, that the champion opposed to me will not be the stoutest or most dexterous, but the heaviest or most shewy, and will readily agree that I have little cause to tremble, when probably I shall find in array against me the *Sovereign* of Mr. Pybus, or a work no less patriotic, the labor of a worthy clergyman, and in praise of better things,—to wit—*bank-notes and strong-beer.*

Many will think that I should have suppressed what I have said; but let them recollect that, amongst those ancient poets who contended for the public prize, each must not only have formed the same determination, (for defects are not usually compared with defects, but are generally contrasted with beauties) but have actually engaged, and that too more openly and personally, in a still more strenuous competition. If my rights had not been refused me, I should not have asserted my claims. Rambling by the side of the sea, or resting on the top of a mountain, and interlining with verses the letters of my friends, sometimes thought how a Grecian would have written, but never what methods he would take to compass popularity. The nearer I approached him, tho' distant still, the more was I delighted. I may add,

> O belle agli occhi miei tende *latine!*
> Aura spira di da voi che mi recrea,

E mi conforta piu piu pur che m'avvicine.

Tasso, *Gerusalemme liberata* [6.104.]

Several of these sketches were obliterated, still more laid aside and lost; various ideas I permitted to pass away, unwilling to disturb, by the slightest action, the dreams of reposing fancy. So little was I anxious to publish my rhapsodies, that I never sate down in the house, an hour at once, for the purpose of composition. Instead of making, or inviting, courtship, I declared with how little I should rest contented. Far from soliciting the attention of those who are passing by, *Gebir* is confined, I believe, to the shop of one bookseller, and I never heard that he had even made his appearance at the window. I understand not the management of these matters, but I find that the writing of a book is the least that an author has to do. My experience has not been great; and the caution which it has taught me lies entirely on the other side of publication. Before I was twenty years of age I had imprudently sent into the world a volume, of which I was soon ashamed. It everywhere met with as much commendation as was proper, and generally more. For, tho' the structure was feeble, the lines were fluent: the rhymes shewed habitual ease, and the personifications fashionable taste. I suffered any of my heroes, the greater part of whom were of a gentle kind, to look on one side thro' the eye of Pity, on the other thro' that of Love; and it was with great delight, for I could not foresee the consequences, that I heard them speak or sing with the lips of soft Persuasion. So early in life, I had not discovered the error into which we were drawn by the Wartons. I was then in raptures with what I now despise. I am far from the expectation, or the hope, that these deciduous shoots will be supported by the ivy of my maturer years. But, without any boast of prudence, I have hung up a motley and paultry skin for my puppies in their snarling playfulness to pull at, that they may not tear in pieces a better and costlier one on which I desire to rest. After all, I do not wonder that they barked at Gebir—he came disguised and in tatters. Still there was nothing to authorize the impertinence with which the publication was treated by the Monthly Reviewer. These are not the faults which he complains of; tho' these might, without his consciousness, have first occasioned his ill-humour. I pity his want of abilities, and I pardon his excess of insolence. The merit is by no means small of a critic who speaks with modesty. For, his time being chiefly occupied, at first, in works fundamentally critical, at least if we suppose him desirous to *learn* before he is ambitious to *teach*, he thinks when he has attained their expressions and brevity, he has attained their solidity and profoundness. He must surely be above what he measures, else how can he measure with exactness? He must be greater, *ex officio*, than the person he brings before him; else how can he stigmatize with censure, or even dismiss with praise? These illusions are indeed so pleasant that to part with them voluntarily is deserving of great applause. In many so strong is the fascination as not to have been broken even by personal attempts at original composition: not tho' the author has grasped even the isolated works of sublime imagination: tho' sinking thro' the dearth of conception, or lost in the deserts of enquiry: tho' pursued by the aggravating hisses, and assailed by the intolerable stings, of obloquy, scorn, and contempt. It is enough if he can enclose in his flimsy web, what, confident as he naturally is, he would be hopeless of reaching in it's flight. Such is the production of these miserable insects, *a month in generating, a moment in existence*. Miserable do I call them! alas, for the wise and virtuous, alas, for human nature! Tho' Justice, in descending on the world again, has given it a partial revolution, so that some who were in sunshine are in shade—some of the highest and most prominent—yet, when I cast my eyes immediately around me, and can discern what passes both in public and in private, I find too often that those are the least miserable who occasion the most misery. For, when any one has done an injury, the power, that enabled him to do it comes back upon the mind, and fills it with such a complacency, as smooths away all the contrition that the action of this injury would have left. And little power is requisite to work much mischief.

APOLOGY
FOR *GEBIR*

Sixty the years since *Fidler* bore
My grouse-bag up the Bala moor;
Above the lake, along the lea
Where gleams the darkly yellow Dee;
Thro' crags, o'er cliffs, I carried there
My verses with paternal care,
But left them, and went home again,
To wing the birds upon the plain.
With heavier luggage half forgot,
For many months they followed not,   10
When over Tawey's sands they came,
Brighter flew up my winter flame;
And each old cricket sang alert
With joy that they had come unhurt.
Gebir! men shook their heads in doubt
If we were sane: few made us out.
Beside one stranger; in his heart
We after held no niggard part.
The songs of every age he knew,
But only sang the pure and true.   20
Poet he was, yet was his smile
Without a tinge of gall or guile.

Such lived, 'tis said, in ages past;
Who knows if Southey was the last?
Dapper, who may perhaps have seen
My name in some late magazine,
Among a dozen or a score
Which interest wise people more,
Wonders if I can be the same
To whom poor Southey augured fame; 30
Erring as usual in his choice
Of one who mocks the public voice,
And fancies two or three are worth
Far more than all the rest on earth.
Dapper, in tones benign and clear,
Tells those who treasure all they hear,
"Landor would have done better far,
Had he observed the northern star;
Or Bloomfield might have shown the way
To one who always goes astray; 40
He might have tried his pen upon
The living, not the dead and gone.
Are turban'd youths and muffled belles
Extinct along the Dardanelles?
Is there no scimitar, no axe?
Daggers and bow-strings, mutes and sacks?
Are they all swept away for ever
From that sky-blue resplendent river?

Do heroes of old time surpass
Cardigan, Somerset, Dundas?   50
Do the Sigæan mounds inclose
More corses than Death swept from those?"
No, no: but let me ask in turn,
Whether, whene'er Corinthian urn.
With ivied Faun upon the rim
Invites, I may not gaze on him?
I love all beauty: I can go
At times from Gainsboro' to Watteau;
Even after Milton's thorough-bass
I bear the rhymes of Hudibras,   60
And find more solid wisdom there
Than pads professor's easy chair:
But never sit I quiet long
Where broidered cassock floats round Young
Whose pungent essences perfume
And quirk and quibble trim the tomb;
Who thinks the holy bread too plain,
And in the chalice pours champagne.
I love old places and their climes,
Nor quit the syrinx for the chimes.   70
Manners have changed; but hearts are yet
The same, and will be while they beat.
Ye blame not those who wander o'er
Our earth's remotest wildest shore,

Nor scoff at seeking what is hid
Within one-chambered pyramid;
Let me then, with my coat untorn
By your acacia's crooked thorn,
Follow from Gades to the coast
Of Egypt men thro' ages lost.   80
Firm was my step on rocky steeps;
Others slipt down loose sandhill heaps
I knew where hidden fountains lay;
Hoarse was their thirsty camels' bray
And presently fresh droves had past
The beasts expiring on the waste.

NOTES

NOTE ON TEXTUAL METHODOLOGY

This version of *Gebir* has been established by using optical
character recognition (OCR) on the digital facsimile of the
1803 edition of *Gebir* and by collating the output with
both the 1803 text and the version of the poem printed in
volume one of *The Poetical Works of Walter Savage Landor*
(ed. Stephen Wheeler, Oxford University Press, 1937). Idio-
syncrasies of spelling and punctuation are respected and
reproduced. Each of Landor's footnotes is reproduced and
none are added. Minor textual changes include: the amend-
ment of "&c." to "etc."; the omission of "End of Book the
First", etc.; and the amending of nested quotation marks
occurring in dialogue from double to single ones. As our
guiding editorial principle, obedience to the copy text
seemed to us more desirable than to embark upon the slippery course of tweaking spellings and punctuation marks.

"Crysaor", "The Phocæans", and "Postscript to *Gebir*"
have been established from Wheeler's versions and col-
lated with digital facsimiles of the originals. "Apology
for *Gebir*" is sourced directly from Wheeler, vol. 3.

This volume follows the convention of shortening the
original title "The Story of Crysaor" to "Crysaor", as Landor
approved of when the poem was collected in a two-volume
omnibus of his work in 1846.

NOTES ON 'GEBIR'

The following appear to be the most substantial variants of the 1831 editions.

I.1-11   These lines are suppressed in the 1831 edition. Line 1 of 1831 reads:

I sing the fates of Gebir. How he dwelt

I.12   Although *Gebir* has never been published as such, Landor evidently preferred this line to commence:

Hear ye the fate of Gebir! [1]

Book IV begins as follows in the 1803 edition:

The king's lone road, his visit, his return,
Were not unknown to Dalica, nor long
The wondrous tale from royal ears delayed.
When the young queen had heard who taught the rites
Her mind was shaken, and what first she asked
Was, whether the sea-maids were very fair,
And was it true that even gods were moved
By female charms beneath the waves profound,
And joined to them in marriage, and had sons—

1. See Kate Field, "The Last Days of Walter Savage Landor, Part II", *The Atlantic*, May 1866. URL: https://www.theatlantic.com/magazine/archive/1866/05/last-days-of-walter-savage-landor-part-ii/628185/

Who knows but Gebir sprang then from the gods!
He that could pity, he that could obey,
Flattered both female youth and princely pride, [...]

VI.188-201 These lines are suppressed in the 1831 edition.

VI.250-299 These lines are suppressed in the 1831 edition.

NOTES ON "THE PHOCÆANS"

By Landor's own account "The Phocæans" is incomplete. Its publication history is such that the poem is understood to exist in four fragments, with a few brief passages inserted on slips of paper in Landor's own copy of a book in which "The Phocæans" was printed.

Two of the fragments were published in *Poetry by the Author of Gebir* (printed 1800, published 1802); two were not published until 1897, long after Landor's death, when Stephen Wheeler published them in *Letters and Other Unpublished Writings of Walter Savage Landor* (London: Richard Bentley & Sons, 1897).

The divisions of the poem's four parts are indicated in the present version by the line numbering, which restarts at the beginning of each section. We follow Wheeler's paragraph divisions. The poem's fragments are as follows.

"Preface". Pp. 121-22. First appeared in *Poetry by the Author of Gebir*.

"From the Phocæans". 668 lines, pp. 123-49. First appeared in *Poetry by the Author of Gebir*. However, lines 660-668, which conclude this section and the speech of Hymneus, are from a slip of paper inserted by Landor into a copy of *Poetry by the Author of Gebir*, according to Wheeler.

"Connecting Link". 15 lines, p. 149. These fifteen lines were inserted in manuscript in a copy of *Poetry by the Author of Gebir* between "From the Phocæans" and "Part of Protis's Narrative". This fragment was first edited by Wheeler in 1897.

"Part of Protis's Narrative". 345 lines, pp. 149-63. In a copy of *Poetry by the Author of Gebir*, Landor appended the following note to the final line of this section:

> There would have been a second part of this poem, narrating a sea-fight with the Carthaginians, recorded in history; then conflicts with the natives. The main difficulty was to devise names for them. An approximation was attempted from the welsh and irish, many of which are harmonious in the termination, an essential in poetry. Druids, Druidesses, Bards, old oaks and capacious wicker baskets were at hand.

In the same volume Landor wrote and deleted the following passage, which he had wished to see inserted in "Advertisement to the Story of Crysaor":

There would have been a second part of the poem entitled The Phocæans, relating the arrival on the coast of Gaul, the first attempt at raising the city of Massilia, and the conflicts with the High Priest of the Druids and the priests and people under his influence. The main difficulty lay in the fabrication of proper names for these impostors and barbarians. Anagrams would look like satire.

"Sequel". 47 lines, pp. 164-65. The MS. of this fragmentary "sequel" was found in Landor's writing-desk, first edited by Wheeler in 1897.

ARGUMENT OF "THE PHOCÆANS"[2]

Dedication to Liberty, the Muses invoked. Persian invasion of Ionia. Fall of Priene. Defying Cyrus and his host, the Phocæans sail to Iberia and seek aid from the king of Tartessus. Speech of Protis their leader and the king's reply. A minstrel from Miletus at the king's bidding recounts the woes of the Tartessians and how these were happily at an end. Their country was invaded by men of Tyre and Sidon, their elders were slain, many of the younger fled to Calpe. Adventures of Hercules in that region. What befel the invaders is next related by the minstrel. Their wives and daughters, performing religious rites on a river bank, were

2. This summary of "The Phocæans" was written not by Landor, but by Wheeler, *The Poetical Works of Walter Savage Landor*, Vol. 1, 1937.

carried off by Nebrissan hill-men. Meanwhile Tartessian fugitives with restored courage had gone back to Tartessus town and overpowered the garrison. Some of the invaders escaped to their ships, a few sought safety inland, the rest were slain. The minstrel then tells how another party of the invaders which left the town, before its recapture, to join wives and daughters beside Lacippo's fount, learnt their fate. Meeting two Nebrissan boys mentioned earlier in the narrative they sacrificed them in revenge for the abduction of their own kindred. Retracing their steps they found Tartessus again in possession of its rightful masters. (Here the minstrel's story and the first fragment of the poem end, and "Part of Protis's Narrative" begins.) Asked by the King of Tartessus to relate the adventures of the Phocæans, their leader, Protis, begins by telling what happened when their country was threatened by a Persian invasion. They consulted the Delphic oracle which foretold toil and trouble. Vainly they sought help from Athens and Sparta. Going back to their sea-port they were victors in a fight with the invaders but, deserted by their allies, they could not hold out on the mainland. Terrified by the threats of Cyrus, the Chians denied them refuge on a nearby island. Some of the Phocæans forgot the oath never to return till molten iron cast into the sea should float on the waves, but the braver set sail for distant lands. This fragment of Protis's speech ends abruptly with their departure, the story of their voyage being left untold.

NOTES ON "APOLOGY FOR GEBIR"

line 1: *Fidler*: a Welsh pony. [Landor's note]

line 11: *Tawey's sands*: a Swansea river. [Landor's note]

lines 1–14: These lines relate the circumstances of *Gebir*'s composition. Landor inadvertently left the manuscript behind in North Wales "on returning from a grouse-shooting expedition on the moors above Bala—where he was possibly a guest of the Price family at Rhiwlas—and 'many months' elapsed before it was forwarded to him at Swansea." (Elwin, Malcolm. *Landor: A Replevin*. London: Archon Books, 1970, pp. 65)

line 50: *Brown, Cambridge, Somerset, Dundas*: General Sir George Brown, Duke of Cambridge; Lord Raglan; Admiral Sir James Whitley Deans Dundas.

line 58: *Gainsboro'*: Thomas Gainsborough (1727–1788), English portrait and landscape painter, draughtsman, and printmaker.

THE EMPYREAN SERIES

about   The Empyrean Series is an imprint of Sublunary
              Editions, dedicated to producing new editions
              of overlooked works from the history of world
              literature.

editors   Jacob Siefring, Joshua Rothes

design   Joshua Rothes

web   sublunaryeditions.com/empyrean

etc.   Empyrean Series titles are printed on acid-free,
              post-consumer paper.

THE EMPYREAN CATALOGUE